HEART *of a* TREE

> *"The struggle itself toward the heights
> is enough to fill a heart."*
>
> 🍁 *Camus*

> *"I leave Sisyphus at the foot of the mountain!
> One always finds one's burden again.
> But Sisyphus teaches a higher fidelity
> that negates gods and raises rocks....
> A universe henceforth without a master
> seems to him neither sterile nor futile.
> Each atom of that stone, each mineral flake
> of that night-filled mountain, in itself forms a world.
> The struggle itself toward the heights
> is enough to fill a heart.
> One must imagine Sisyphus happy."*
>
> 🍁 *Camus*

HEART
of a
TREE

NEW POEMS WRITTEN IN 2010

WILLIAM HOLLIS

with photographs by ANDREA BALDECK

HAWKHURST BOOKS

Poems Copyright © 2011 by William Hollis
Photographs Copyright © 2011 by Andrea Baldeck
ISBN 978-0-9748304-8-3
Hawkhurst Books, 6122 Butler Pike, Blue Bell, PA 19422
www.williamhollis.com

CONTENTS

Hollow Tree / 5
Buckeye / 8
Syntax of Destruction / 10
In the Senator's Pool / 14
Holiday with a Friend / 15
Touches of Young Sex / 16
Late Lute / 20
Wine, Sun, and Words / 21
Heart of a Tree / 22
Trees as a Part of Me / 26
Light in an Aging Heart / 27
Crumbs and Buber / 28
Katsura / 30
Life's Echo from Pascal / 32
Listening for What It's All About / 34
Pretty Boy / 35
One of the Guys / 36
Empty Space / 37
The Rise of His Voice / 38
Spinach Pie / 39
Growing Old on the Bay / 40
With Many Girls / 44
Retired Whores / 46
A Walk Through a Cemetery / 53
Japanese Maples / 54
Late Party / 56
Question and No Answer / 57
Black Bottle of Words / 58
Subject Matter / 60
Brass Poem / 61
Wonder of Winds / 62
Alphabattery of Friends / 64
To Hear Her / 65
Verbal Coins / 66
Blue Atlas Cedar / 68
Too Soon to Quit / 70
Talking with Gulls / 74
Old Tin Box / 75
Where Do We Go / 76
Understanding / 78
Edgy Friend / 80

Lack of Knowing / 82
Death of a Lime Tree / 84
Ash in a Found Poem / 85
Graveyard Wind / 86
Making Notes / 87
    Bald Cypress / 88
Voices Right Here / 90
Restlessness / 91
Once Upon a Time / 92
Last Notes / 93
An Old Man Remembers Sex / 94
Bach's Cello Suites / 96
Old Ones / 98
Wild Horses Dance to *Swan Lake* / 100
Friendship That Failed / 101
    Knot / 102
Old Teacher's Lament / 104
Blues for a Friend / 105
Blue Rocker / 106
Blue Search for the Truth / 107
Blue Regrets / 108
Where Music Begins / 109
Not Sure / 110
Fragile Friendship / 111
Just Friends / 112
What Might Have Been / 113
    Rot / 114
Sharing With a Friend / 116
Gator Threats / 117
Dismissal of an Atheist / 118
A Birthday / 120
Memories in an Old Rocker / 122
Notes from Bach / 123
Not Time / 124
Tales for Me / 125
Arguments / 126
Word for Another Poem / 128
After 80 Years / 129
    Author in the Heart of a Tree / 130
    A Brief Biography / 131
    Books / 133

SYNTAX OF DESTRUCTION

I

On an island in Budapest where the world
had come to a time without rest,
we sat and talked for an afternoon
in languages I only half understood,
if even that, certainly not Hungarian;
but in that afternoon, quietly,
we left words scattered with little hope
but with warm gestures for friends we might
or might not have met before, with whom,
for a few hours, we heard birds
quarrel in trees as passions of a river
fled by, murmuring it would be all right,
it too would be gone and repeat itself;
and when the men in dark suits passed,
I was taught to slide into silence with no change
of expression, just a bit of patience
until they too had passed and the sun
slid through trees with a sudden marking
of the end of another day where strangers
might brush with pleasure against each other.

II

I do remember, after fifty-five years,
the polished pistol I carried to work,
loaded and ready suddenly to use,
that, luckily, I never had to pull
and, when I left the army, was left
lying on a master sergeant's desk;
and there was one I pulled from my father's
underwear drawer one night as a stranger
bumped around the yard in the dark
after mother, scared, had gone looking for it

but couldn't untangle it from boxer shorts;
I had never seen it before, but the stranger
disappeared before we did more than peer
through one of the rattling windows;
and a day later, after father's return
from a business trip, the pistol disappeared,
unused, and was nowhere to be found;
with both parents dead, we searched in vain
to see if it might be pulled from a drawer
and taken home for some future use.

III

At twenty-two I often slept on a pile of hay
on a ridge while wearing a gray flannel suit
and a backpack that held a bottle of wine
and a copy of Tolstoy's *War and Peace*
in an edition small enough for little weight;
and on those nights as, without food,
not even a piece of warm cheese,
I watched stars and listened to silence
through blowing wind, waiting for something
to pull me to what I did not know,
which might be nothing more than a dream
or the distant sound of bells, perhaps
from one of the steeples I had seen
below me as I climbed and looked for a place
to rest, like the barn where old men
played guitars and softly sang
of those who were dead, who did not return;
and a few of us, the age of grandsons,
listened and slept little until dawn
when left to wander off on our own.

IV

I did not climb trees when I was a child,
except during those years when my father
came home from work and turned on
a radio full of serious voices who told us
that 20,000 more had been killed
in a battle fought somewhere, perhaps Africa;
and I would slam out the door and climb
to the top of a grapefruit tree where I
could shake the limbs and not hear the news,
the horror being so soberly announced
by H. V. Kaltenborn, an escape that has
not worked in the decades since I lost
the burst of energy it takes to climb;
though, as years pass, I learn
to keep the television closed in a closet
and a recording of some Irish street music
from the 16th century filling the room
instead of news—because that world
doesn't change, always more bleedings
and bodies to drive me up a grapefruit tree.

V

I always knew there was somewhere else
I should have gone before a ticket
left me sitting in the sun waiting for a bus,
waiting to see if I could get
beyond the valley, the usual place
I had to go and so too rarely
got anywhere else, especially those mountains
I'd always seen fading beyond me;
perhaps it was my fault I was left waiting,
not knowing what I'd do if it didn't come,

as it often didn't in those untimely days
when not even a limping warrior could know
if he'd get home before darkness fell
and left the bus stalled on the edge of town
stinking up an unknown neighborhood,
leaving us to stumble around unlit tanks
and to mutter something about a beer
and what we'd do if we ran the buses,
and how we didn't want to be there anyway,
wherever we were in that lost valley.

VI

There was nothing left to argue about
on a final weekend with little to say;
and even her mother sighed and suggested
we find where a new path might lead
while her father slipped into dead silence;
and I wondered what a real relationship
might bring, where lead, with what feelings,
as, for years, I wandered quiet times
this side of distant wars, never sure
just what I felt, though I listened carefully,
trying to find what the syntax of destruction
might be, how I might find answers
to questions that recur with every breath,
with silence or an emotional rant
that would carry a pair of us into rich
structuring of words, ideas and feelings,
into a structural reality of poems,
that moment when the phrase she used
would echo the one I could always add
as richness to a world we would build together.

IN THE SENATOR'S POOL

I was young, very young and eager,
and the senator was very old,
but he gave lovely parties at his pool
where, at twenty-four, I met
the first girl for whom I stumbled
with what I thought might be love.
She raised her head above the senator's
water and said how glad she was
to meet, just let her finish her laps
and she would come and talk some more.
The senator smiled, perhaps because
he knew my father and knew that I
might someday hold a small fortune,
a bit of knowledge I did not have;
but why he cared for Anne and saw
her more than me, I never knew—
and saw him only twice again
before he died, and do not think
that she and I for the next five years
even spoke his name as we'd try to find
just why it was she only remembered
the blue-eyed guy who was, she said,
so much better looking than I, so tall
and fun to love, though he got married
to someone else, and she and I
kept arguing over possibilities
of what we had having found each other,
as she left me sleeping on the rug
in either her apartment or mine;
and never again did we speak
of the old guy, the old senator
who brought us together for a long space
of argumentation and rich lust
that never lead us anywhere
but is something much to be remembered.

HOLIDAY WITH A FRIEND

Yes, yes…, a week from yesterday
and 'Bah humbug' to all the *fal-de-ral;*
but what we look forward to is light in the eyes
of people like you! Yes, yes.
Light can appear in eyes even if they
are full of tears, for tears, after all, are among
the most convincing manifestations of life.

Our snow was beautiful, arriving heavily
on Saturday, glittering into ice on Sunday
and, still today, Tuesday,
lighting a field here and a stretch of lawn there,
which, from my computer chair,
I watch, right over there, see, right out
between here and the Japanese cherries.

We will see you, I assume and hope,
between now and when you leave to be
with your friend, which sounds like a good idea,
as would a visit from an old friend
who was here for three hours a couple
of weeks ago and we talked of little else
except the plausibility of death.

TOUCHES OF YOUNG SEX

1

Was I ever young enough to have played a silly joke
on the pretty girls in class who never gave a damn?
Or did I grow too quickly old with restlessness
at what the future might bring to me or even them?
There was a quiet one who soon became a nun,
and one who, decades later, will occasionally write;
and then will disappear as she always has.

For twenty years at a time I'll not receive a word,
and then she'll fill me in on the death of her companion
and seem to need, of course, a little cheering up.
But who am I after so many years to find a joke
that might relieve the pain of age or death with a shrug?
We never know as a child whether years will end
with tears or laughter, or a falling loss of memory.

2

Before I could even imagine what sex might be about,
I spent my Saturday afternoons scrubbing floors
and sighed when one of the pretty girls in the neighborhood
would wander in with her mother to buy a ham for dinner;
and I would try, perhaps a little desperately,
to joke and hold her sad attention that even in class
never seemed to drift my way unless I recited poems.

"Hello," she'd say without a smile and drift away;
and I'd return to mop the floors and wonder why
she never paid attention, even in class when the teacher
would ask her to respond to the book I'd reported on
and she would giggle without a bit of light in her eyes
and I would sigh and wonder what the trouble was,
and wonder if I should write a greeting before the end.

3

There was a girl I dated with a chill, in spite
of warm Floridian nights when, even if we parked
on banks of the lake, we'd feel the wind and hear the cough
of a gator with a splash at the edge of water and weeds
that made us grit our teeth and wonder if it could be
a warning like those our mothers gave that we should go
back to another place where lights were always cleaving.

Years later I saw her when back for my father's death,
and we sat for awhile beside the lake and sounds of gators,
and talked of marriages that had fallen down the bank
into muddy splashes of a world we'd not expected.
"It was here," she said, "long ago and we did not know,
though we wondered if we'd ever know or ever find
a way to a world where predators would not linger."

4

So many wars since then, so much destruction that
leaves me wandering byways I had forgot
and wondering where others are, the ones who turned
away to save themselves from frigid air.
Perhaps chills I felt on hot afternoons came
from poems I loved to chant or music that was meant
to pull into one's heart and whisper of a future love.

I've only begun to find myself as I approach again
the sliding call of alligators that I avoided back then,
so many years ago; though now I know they are there,
always there, to push aside the hopes I had that I
would find an easy way around the lake and up
the hills until I learned to laugh or cry with all
the freedom I didn't know, back then, I would have.

5

Why not, I said over and over again; why not,
I said so many times the words became thematic notes
within clusters of words, an orchestration
of life, at least for me, especially when I'd strike a pair
of notes as if on drums I made from hollow trees
that rotted and fell from grandfather's orchard
and echoed over and over, Why not? Why not?

I woke to the words for an early morning's confab
with just myself, wondering Why not? Why not?
after a night we had walked the hills and watched moon
bedim the stars, until an angry dog drove us away.
Why not, I said, and crumbled toast and tried to make sure
my grandmother did not ask: "Why what? Why do
you mutter? Were you with that crazy girl last night?"

6

She wasn't beautiful, not like the girls who leapt
and shouted for boys to hit their balls and run;
her smile was low and saved for a moment when Bach
made an organ reverberate across the room
and down the hall her father had built just for it.
She didn't play for others, but for herself and me;
and then she'd drive across the state to hear me play.

And we would argue about what Mozart might
have done if he had come along a little after Liszt;
and then we'd drive out to the Gulf and talk
or argue for an hour or so, and I would long
to touch her arm, to whisper at her ear, to touch
whatever it was that seemed so small within her body;
but all we did was talk, all we ever did was talk.

7

We spent an afternoon on the trail up Bear Mountain
and listened to the cough of an angry deer and echoes
from distant traffic. But why was it I who held back,
why did I push my hands into thorns that lined
the trail, why did I gather a couple of walking sticks,
ignore the brush of her arm, the smile she dropped
at the top of the trail as we looked back down the river?

And there, in a dome of distance, an emptiness of time,
a city that might one day be ours, that might be what
had never let us touch, had kept us in a world
where sex was just the subject of another play,
perhaps with two like us, only free to wander
when headed up a mountain path beyond the city,
beyond the touching we thought would be for us.

8

But I got older and found the words of love
and found that I could stroke and even laugh
with age and wait, as she climbed her mountains,
to laugh and watch as days grow short, and wonder
if the past has been as necessary as I thought, as I
have written on a set of dark and windy days not far
from the end in a tone that isn't meant to be sad.

No, not all so sad, for some of us still laugh,
even when we stumble up the stairs and sigh
and remember the path that led across the Alps
where it was fun to touch whenever we could
and a loss to find that touching is often just a hug;
but memory is alive and I play these words
as if they were still whisperings of seduction.

LATE LUTE

It's late, and a lute tries to pull
me from the indifference I feel
to darkness that closes down the house,
to silence the tides have left here
on the edge of a swamp I can not see,
not now, not after the sun has fallen
and we've had wine and supper.

I can not tell if the lute is old
or from the mountains of Tennessee.
It's clean and lonely as I listen,
distracted now by a few words
that suddenly begin to fall
from the edge of sleep across a page,
reaching for a bit of your awareness.

When the sun fell an hour ago
I thought I'd sit here quietly
and find rhythms of what I've passed
since I aged and settled into a chair,
six or eight books beside me,
waiting to fill the emptiness
of the heart with possibilities of hope.

Is this the lute I heard in the mountains
a half century ago, when young
and unaware of what it was
I heard? Though I must admit
I feel again the pressure from tears,
something inside that says, "Listen,
it's here, in the echo of this lute".

What's here I do not know: the heart
perhaps of what I've given a life to find
and never recognized, never pulled out
and said, with a sigh, that this was it;
it's here, even if I never know
what the *it* may be—a tonality that
gives answer to the longing of the heart.

WINE, SUN, AND WORDS

We sip the wine and watch the sun
slowly sink toward the edge of life;
we spend the afternoon with words,
some of which are here in a near-by poem,
some of which have gone out to friends,
words that carry a bit of who we are,
words that might hold out a hope
that lingers with brilliant colors of the sun.

The sinking sun brings her to words
that have the brilliance of photographs,
while I, who've spent a lifetime pushing
through trash barrels looking for words,
listen with jealousy to what she's found
here in an afternoon as the sun
pulls eyes to a distance we've never seen
until now when the only distraction is wine.

It's moments like this that bring us closer;
and I lift my glass to the edge of hers
and they touch at the moment the sun flattens
across the bay, leaving a sheen
the color of wine across the sky,
leaving us, for a moment, without words,
with only their echo in the shift of tides
and a chill of pleasure across our backs.

HEART OF A TREE

1

In the heart of a tree, an old apple
with a few leaves and rotten fruit,
we found, on a summer day, four kittens
abandoned by an old feral mother, gone
and never seen again, four kittens
there in the heart of the tree whining
in hunger and perhaps an early fear,
four newborns we fed and tried to save,
tried to place in homes for survival;
but not even the mother reappeared,
an old Maine cat that now was gone
as soon were the kittens she had left
behind, as soon was the aging tree
that rotted more and blew down.

2

A tree has a heart that can be found;
we have the top of a table carved
by an artist from the heart of a maple.
It's long been stained by glasses of wine;
though occasionally the artist will visit,
sigh at the damage that has been done
and remind us how old the tree was
before he found it sliced in a barn
and polished it for tables and chairs;
the heart of a treasure not left to rot
like trees that are left to rot and hollow
as homes for hawks or squirrels and cats;
the heart of a tree can last for centuries,
if we are willing to hold it close.

3

When I was a child we watched for trees
where gators and snakes slid in and out,
and mother, who was hardly a feral cat,
would scare me shitless by crying out
that I would lose an arm if not careful—
that gators would suddenly reappear
and take hold of whatever splashed
or whatever they could reach before dark;
and then it would be dark and I'd be gone,
somewhere down there where rotting hearts
had disappeared among remnants of trees
right there where a serpent suddenly slid
through a last lingering fall of light,
a serpent in the heart of an old swamp tree.

4

Not far from where we live now, a tree
survives as a cave on the edge of a creek,
all limbs now gone, not a branch or a leaf,
just what was once a very large trunk,
a great pilaster of time that slowly
over hundreds of years dropped its life
and took the shape, the life of a cave
where one might hide, might stare out
at a world that slowly rotted and got worse,
leaving only an afternoon where I
might stand at the heart of the lingering past,
letting those hundreds of years scar
my fingers, lingering with photographic
passion in the memory of that afternoon.

5

Can the heart of a tree linger with me
as the crotch where this limb joins another,
swells with pain and brings me close
to falling when winds come close to pushing
harder than the *Times* with the morning news?
It isn't easy to stay upright
when rocks of a cliff are sliding with mud
that takes old trees with them, down,
down where villages have been lost,
down where, we're told, another age
will sweep away the last of hope.
I've hugged a dying tree and wept;
I've hoped an artist caught that heart
and left us with possibilities.

6

Ah, yes, my friends, the heart of the tree
is with me yet; and lingers as it did
when I was a child and didn't know
it could and would entirely disappear.
The old apple tree is gone, but another
ages and opens itself to the light,
to another feral cat or family
of squirrels, or these memories I keep
to share with any of the *you* who read
these small sketches on a cold afternoon
when I find that picture of me in a tree
like one of the worn spots any life
can get as time goes on and winds
slam at shutters and leave them to rattle.

7

Sometimes one must deliberately cut
at the heart of the past, if not the whole
then the part that termites love to gnaw;
take it out, even if at the heart,
and maybe for awhile we'll eat the fruit
and find that, yes, there was something there,
something that might help us find a way
among bits of human history
that had survived, for awhile survived
in spite of water tides that rose
and fell again, carrying so much
of what we thought would rescue us
and leave us with a rhythmic heart
to carry us like music to a final cadence.

8

There's a female Buddha at the local museum,
a thousand years and still a smile;
she flourishes as the heart of a tree
that grew in the courtyard of a temple;
she was carved from the heart of that tree
and took the heart and brought it here
for us to watch during an afternoon
when we thought there was nothing else to do
and only then found we had grown
like trees that flourish until they rot,
the circular richness of what could be
if we'd but pay attention and smile
and see that in her corpse there might
just be the clue of what it's all about.

TREES AS A PART OF ME

Why is the tree so much a part of what I am?
Is it because I saw it fall in heavy wind
or even lift itself and enter the house next door,
roots first, intrusive, a battering ram from the past?
Or are they like the monsters I dreamt of as a child,
a group of them in the middle of a mangrove swamp
that seemed to wait and trail me through afternoons?
Or was it the tree in which a turkey was hung to die
or where a wild boar's throat was slit and he was left
to drain the future of where I might end up, for it
was there, just out the window, where I hid from the death
of those battalions I didn't want to hear about?

I've dreamt of trees and dreamt I climbed to the very top
of a pine that swished through afternoons of heavy wind;
and there was a dream in which I wandered through a forest
that stretched across an island and climbed a tree or two
and explored the hiding place of feral cats, of foxes
and ghosts of indians and slaves trying to lose themselves.
I used to scrub about among rotting branches
that were not part of a passing dream, real trees,
to see if I could find the splinters of a bone,
the last of those who faced death before I came
and brought my own potentiality of growth
and rot and death through long futures of the world.

LIGHT IN AN AGING HEART

What can I do to turn the light around
and find the pathway through a local park
I used to know when I could not have known
that darkness on a mountain top would bring
a brightness of the stars into my heart?

And then today my daughter called again
to ask if I remember where the path
had slipped on down the hill to the river's edge,
where we had wandered when she was a child
and laughed at possibilities of fear.

How do we know, how can we possibly know
where real denial of the past may lie,
where all the hope we had would linger on
and push us from reflections of the sun
to far and sweeping glitters of the stars?

"It's late, too late," I told her when she called;
"it's said the path is no longer there;
a storm swept through and blew down trees."
It's like so much of life we've tried to live,
the crush of stones's a nightmare from the past.

But watch, I say, the moon out there is full
and rises through leafless branches of an oak,
while over there the dying sun reflects
a pale dramatic light on lingering clouds—
so even with an aging heart I smile.

CRUMBS AND BUBER

1

On a cold afternoon when sky clears
and bright light falls across the screen
of my computer, I think of old friends
and quotations from books that fall apart.

Yes, right here to my left, Pascal and Buber,
Camus and lingering crumbs
from an earlier indulgence, surround me
in the way they have for many decades.

Having finished the cookies, I opened Buber
and pushed through disintegrating paper,
pausing to read a quotation circled
by flowing ink when we used ink that flowed.

2

Funny, because I had recently written
a poem with a scattering of passages from Pascal,
a poem that should be located somewhere
near a poem that may fall from these lines.

The challenge, of course, is to find a way
that will lead to or from the Buber
of whom, after all, I've used so much,
including a whole volume or two of letters.

It was he who carried me into another world
with words that slipped me far beyond
the cautious world where I was born, the past
that sent me into a world where I would stumble.

3

"How can we muster the strength to address
an incubus by his right name," he says
somewhere, "as long as a ghost lurks inside
the *I* that has been robbed of actuality?"

"How can buried power to relate," he says
with sense, "be resurrected in an *I* in which
a vigorous ghost appears hourly to stamp down
the debris under which this power lies?"

And then he closes, as I read it: "How is an *I*
to collect himself as long as his mania seems to chase
ceaselessly around an empty circle? How is anyone
to behold freedom if he or she still dwells with Caprice."

4

The clarity of the afternoon darkens;
an early frost falls across the field out back.
If I am to read more Buber or find more words,
I'll have to find the artificial light switch.

That's why the *I* is often left alone
in a dark room at the top of the house
waiting for a *you* from out there, somewhere,
suddenly to respond, "Yes, yes, I hear you."

Maybe I am the *you* for someone else;
maybe I am the *you* to whom he murmured
as he left the stage for the last time, but paused
and almost smiled and nodded at the books I held.

LIFE'S ECHO FROM PASCAL

From the beginning, I've known that
"We sail over a vast expanse, ever uncertain,
ever adrift, carried to and fro"; and then
my music teacher, when I was 10, gave me
this quotation in a Russian I could never understand:
"Those who can only play on ordinary instruments
get no music out of this one."
Only later did I find the spirit of this quotation
in "Playing upon the human organ, we think
we are playing on an ordinary organ.
This flesh is indeed an organ,
but fantastic, changeable, variable…."

I found the following back in high school:
"One must know oneself;
though it may not help to discover truth,
it at least helps to rule one's life —
and what can be better?"
And I threw this one at my father,
to his indifference: "…quite as great capacity
is needed to attain the Nothing as the All…."
And a lovely old lady gave me these words
in her attempt at intellectual seduction:
"We are something, but we are not all…."
The best painting I've done is of these words.

At Princeton, I used the following quotation twice,
which may be why I never finished a graduate degree:
"Finally, others tire themselves to death
in studying many things — not in order
to make themselves wiser, but only to display
their knowledge, and these are the most foolish
of the lot, for they know how foolish they are."
This actually is what I first thought of
after receiving an early e-mail letter:
"It is natural for the mind to believe,
and for the will to love (or even desire);
so, failing real objects, they must fix on false ones."

And, of course, always, there is an echo of
"He who does not see the world's futility
is himself most futile." So, even more,
I find myself saying "…we seek bustle and noise
to drown thought and divert ourselves."
And this next Pascal has lingered longest
in my life, always somewhere on my desk
or on the fridge where drawings
by the children were regularly hung:
"I have often said that man's unhappiness
arises from one thing only, namely
that he cannot abide quietly in one room."

Perhaps most of my poems have been
about encounters with self and others
because of such words as "We wish for truth,
and find in ourselves only incertitude.
We wish for happiness, and find
only misery and death.
We are incapable of not wishing for truth
and happiness, and are incapable
either of certitude or of happiness."
And thus I return to the beginning,
where "We sail over a vast expanse,
ever uncertain, ever adrift, carried to and fro."

LISTENING FOR WHAT IT'S ALL ABOUT

When, once again, I hear that Mimi is dead,
I have, since I was a boy and listened to
the radio on Saturday afternoons,
or later when I wandered along the Seine
and up to the high seats of the Opera House,
trying, with wonder or curiosity,
to find what I might really be all about,
beginning to think I'd never know, that all
I'd know when music begins to sound this way
is that there's nothing else to know or do
but wait to feel the back of my neck as it
begins to quiver, knowing that if it does,
at least the music will have been played well
with voices to convince me that the tenor
is good enough to make me think he cares;
and even if I say I never cry,
I feel tears crush from my eyes and feel
silence surround each note, as it does
now as I try to quote this poem and listen
and know at any moment her voice will slip
away and he will have to pretend that she
is sleeping even as his friends go quiet,
go suddenly silent, and the violins
softly edge at the afternoon, and I,
knowing that it is coming at any moment,
those last chords and the double syllables
crying "Mimi," and the orchestra falls
as do my words as I try to see through tears
and ignore applause and cheers and bravi as I
look out at snow-covered fields, blue sky,
dark shadows in the corners of the orchard,
and look around and in and sigh again,
as I have done for almost eighty years,
listening for what it might be all about.

PRETTY BOY

The pretty boy who used to cheer the room
seems more and more to slip through memory
and leave us to wonder how we never saw
dark shadows falling from his aging hips.

Even those of us who much prefer to sleep
with the opposite sex can easily admit
he was a pretty boy who cheered the table
through drinks and dinner and a lot of talk.

And now we find that he has stolen piles
of money from friends who laughed with him,
who smiled and laughed and wondered how he did
the things they thought he did, like helping kids.

We wonder how the pretty boy will hold
his own now that the shadows are revealed
and the game has come loose and we can see
just what it is we never saw before.

We feel the sadness of a charm that's lost,
pain that comes when admiration is lost;
and we can think of nothing else to say,
no solace or revenge in heart or mind.

Perhaps we'll learn to hold ourselves back,
to keep our eyes a little more alert for what
might leave us with sour and shameful pain
at what we thought was admiration for a friend.

ONE OF THE GUYS

He often came to lunch at the tavern,
where beer after beer would follow without
anything to eat; and then he'd disappear
even if he was supposed to do some work
in our barn to keep it from falling down.

After the third beer he'd start to tell
a tale of emails his wife was sending
to a guy on the other side of town;
then suddenly he'd seem to know he was out
of line and should slam shut the door.

The guys at the bar would shrug and eat
their sandwiches, regretting that it was time
to return to work on one of the houses
in the neighborhood; and he would shrug
and say goodbye in a hesitant voice.

One day, a little earlier than usual,
he arrived at the bar for bourbon on ice
and mumbled something about sticking a knife
in his wife's belly and leaving her
on the floor of his room beside the computer.

And that's the moment the usual guys
arrived, just before three police officers
came rushing in and grabbed his arms,
stuttering that he was under arrest
for stabbing his wife who was still alive.

It was rather quiet after the police cars
pulled away; and for awhile we looked down
and sipped our beers: "Where are his children?"
someone said and we sighed, and silence
filled the bar and fresh beers were poured.

EMPTY SPACE

If you are not here and not there,
then where are you? I'm not sure,
for you seem to have slipped away,
slipped into another circumstance.
It's easy to do; we've found that out
when suddenly we no longer hear
the voice we know, the one with whom
we exchanged those endless stories, some
of which were almost true, had really
happened, or so we told ourselves
and laughed and waited for response
that might bring a happy echo.

But now that's gone or you are gone,
not there where I thought you might linger
while I yawned and used the loo
and came back in to tell a tale
I was sure that you had never heard.
But you are gone. You are gone again,
and I'm left to wonder just who might care,
for the sun's still up, the limbs of the trees
are still; and silence presses the window,
and a few early flowers bloom
as I wonder just why you had to leave,
leaving an empty space with me.

THE RISE OF HIS VOICE

We listen with attention to what he says
and hear the heated memory of pain.
"It isn't I," he says as he tries to hold back
the push that rises in his voice, that lurks
at the edge of what he really seems to be.

But what is it we really push to hear,
and what's the explication of what we hear?
It's a lifetime trying to release itself
and trying to say, "I'm free, I really am,
if you'll just give me time to find myself."

We feel attracted by his intensity
that must be generated by his search;
it's magnetic, perhaps a little dangerous;
but it really seems to be just who he is,
though the rising voice insists it isn't he.

It's a little like the music he plays
as he vibrates the strings across a box
and gives rise to an afternoon with a dance,
his body rising with a cry that reaches
for a song, his hope for resolution of pain.

SPINACH PIE

I love mysteries, which may be why now,
so late, I try a collection of canti
with lots of unidentified cats; but you can
be sure that I have never served
a spinach pie for lunch or dinner,
though perhaps I once ate a toasted one
with a mug of coffee at a diner somewhere
along the highway that stretches between
Mendocino, California, and Brunswich, Georgia.

But this never would have been done
with my daughter, whom I didn't know you knew,
unless you're courting her for your son
when he wanders out of prison, looking
for spinach pie and an unattached
woman with money. So, you see, my dear,
I have no idea what you mean or might
have meant or whom you might have been
writing to about that spinach pie.

GROWING OLD ON THE BAY

1

Bay waters are still and clear this afternoon
as clouds roll across a flat horizon,
there west of me, and reflect in these waters,
dramatic, unreal, more like a painting than I
could have imagined as I sit here on a balcony
that overlooks the living room and out
to salt water, not 20 feet away at low tide,
while long-necked birds, like those that fed around
Lake Hollingsworth when I was a child,
seem to wonder why that old crazy guy
with three legs, including a cane, has not
been out to throw them a fist of stale bread
since he came out under a previous sun
and left a pile of crumbs on the lonely dock.

2

While my companion is flying with cameras
up and down the waterways in a bouncy plane,
I have been writing more of my latest drabbles,
here on this inside balcony, and suddenly
think of old friends who occasionally write, who live
and die without ever filling me with stories,
without giving me a picture of the years
we've lived in separate worlds that are worlds apart,
until I remember her face and find she peers
through cloudy words I find at moments like this
as I sit and watch the dying sun and find
I'm suddenly a lifetime away from those
with whom I spent my early years, a lifetime
in truth since she is the only one I know alive.

3

At least my mind, if awkwardly, works;
and half the memory still lingers there,
though even that may need a little prodding
from time to time, for now you seem to be
on the other side of a cliff, which isn't because,
I hope, you are iller than you were or feeling
too much of your age which is the same as mine;
and then I look down from the deck at the top
of the house and watch a long black snake slip
through wild grass and into swamp nettles
and, I suppose, into the bay, and wonder
if you were here would you take a shot
at him as he disappears into the swamp,
leaving a blank place in faded memory.

4

I sit here on the inside balcony
at my computer screen, seeing if I
can't finish another sonnet before it's time
to grab a glass of wine and head to the dock
to watch the sun, which we might just see tonight
as it swells, brightens, and turns briefly green
and sinks over there beyond the bay; then words
from you arrive and I finish the sonnet and type
this note for you before I rush downstairs
to face the most discouraging thing about fall,
the increasingly early setting of the sun;
so this is why the note for you got twisted
into a poem, this sonnet that's just for you,
if not for all of us, until the next one.

5

If I were younger and more mobile, I'd love,
when we get home, to drive into town and see
if, for a half an hour, I might make you,
if not laugh, at least grin. For look, my friend,
there have been many articles recently
about chemo-brain, one of the worst
reactions the body can have to a stinker process
like you've been through in the last year. So I
have settled at my computer, overlooking
a bay I watch turn blue as the sun rises
and all I can sing is a bay-holler curse
at fate that drops refinement in its choice;
and all I can add is a feeble verbal hug,
which hangs here like the tail of a sad puppy.

6

More and more, I realize, the older I get,
how little I really know of what I'd like
to know: for example, I have recently started
a serious exploration of field-holler blues
that I grew up with but never knew about,
for I was always playing Mozart; some
of it is very good, some terrible;
and I just picked up, last week, the reissue
of Ledbetter or Leadbelly recordings
for Lomax: a bit too slippery in this cleaned-up
version of what, as prison blues, should have
been harsher, and probably were; but I never knew
what brutality lurked in those who sang and those
who cracked the whip and laughed in brutal scorn.

7

It's funny, though, but I do enjoy, with a deep
and gutsy pleasure the very process of writing;
and now, since I've thrown medications away
(which dulled the brain), I enjoy it even more
and look out at possibilities of death
almost at any moment, of course; one can't
get to this age without confronting that—
so maybe this is what has driven me
for the last few years to juggle so many words:
a large set of canti is almost done and a memoir
that looks back to find where words
began for all this stuff. While some of it
will look like prose, I try to push until
it sounds like verse, like a beating of the heart.

8

We bought a rather ugly house among
the pines between two bays and furnished it,
the private working parts of it, like home,
even with complex computers like those at home.
I'm much too old to drive this far these days,
so we fly from there to here or get our Steve
to drive from door to door; and then I sit
and do here without a ring of the telephone
what I do there, except for two things:
just once a day we go to a fisherman's shack
and buy fresh-caught seafood for the day's dinner;
and then, a half hour before the sun will set,
we pour a glass of wine and sit and sip
and watch until the sun has slipped away.

WITH MANY GIRLS

I

Does he remember how often he came for lunch,
or when we met at the diner for breakfast and talk
about the lovely girl he had just met?
He'd talk with such enthusiasm, then pause
and catch his breath and admit it was nothing new;
but I knew—we all knew—and waited for his
return because we knew he'd have a tale,
another tale to tell. "The brightest yet,"
he'd say and make a careful time to come
and give an introduction. He actually did,
oh, once or twice, before she would disappear
or bring a charge, before she would leave again
with someone else and we would meet at the diner
and he would moan and groan until he laughed
and admitted he had a date that night with another
who was really lovely, he'd suddenly say and smile
as groans and moans would disappear; but then
he'd leave for somewhere, perhaps with her, just gone,
and I would think of him and wonder where—
and friends would call and ask if I had heard.

2

The other day I passed his house that now
seems utterly deserted, crouched behind
the hedge he left untrimmed, or so it seems,
to swelter in unseasonable heat or even
wither with the frost. It's been that long.
It has. Oh yes, we do keep track, or try;
and words arrive, a few at a time, that say
he's found a girl in Buenos Aires or Rome
who has the space to let him stay when she
is gone, to let him bring a stranger in—
one, so someone said, who's left the street
and mixes drinks at a bar in the neighborhood.
I don't believe I've ever met again
even one of the few he brought for introductions;
but once in a while we hear a tale that says
the one who went to jail is out again,
though no one knows just whom she sees to pay
the bills, though maybe she's the one, this time,
that holds him once again for a little longer
than all the others through all these many years.

RETIRED WHORES

1

Our island is overrun with heavy
middle-aged women with bright blonde hair
and dramatically over-painted eyes,
an island where whores from Baltimore
or Ocean City retire,
driving aging, elegant sports cars,
and work as gatekeepers at island parks
or bartenders at better bars.

When Istvan, my tall Hungarian
caregiver, is driving,
they flutter their eyelids and laugh;
when I am driving, they glance
at my old-man's *get-in-free card*,
and, I can swear, sneer.

2

When they serve a beer and are waiting
for a tip, they laugh and hint
at long stories they might like to share.
They certainly beat the female donors
or wives of donors
at fund-raising festivities in the city,
where proprieties still cough
with reminders of what should be done.

Since I'm too old for anything else,
I like to stick them in an occasional poem,
if not at the center, then somewhere
hanging out in an early stanza,
opening up possibilities
for something amusing later on.

3

Well, actually, today, sitting
in a local, eating raw oysters
and watching bright aging blondes
retired from the streets of Baltimore
celebrate their freedom,
I think of the bar at home
and my friends there, and wonder
if they are holding on.

I hope they are feeling well
in spite of a world that squeezes,
when it can, anyone it can,
in any way it can—
that's what they found out,
these hefty blondes.

4

Back when they worked in one
of the strip joints down at the shore,
dancing around a pole,
they tried to get geeky kids like me,
fresh out of school
with too much time in libraries,
and now in the army for awhile,
to put down our books and laugh.

Those books were actually
a bogus show by us
to stir up that world
that seemed so overheated—
not that we had much of an idea
of what an overheated world was all about.

5

And there was that night when Uta,
a tall, handsome pole dancer
from Berlin and Baltimore,
retired and living on our tropic island,
tried to leap off the deck,
as if she would dance her way
down among stones
where the sea crashed.

The rest of us read poems
and poured wine and would
have been satisfied if she had danced
and stripped and interrupted the poems,
even though they were mine,
being read by other wanderers.

6

Though now too old to wander over
to East Baltimore Street, much less
to her club, closed by the mayor,
who had already run off
with another large blonde,
the wanderers gathered on the deck
would not have cared
if she had stripped or jumped.

They had been there and done that,
and much else besides…;
and now, as one of the run-away docs
sighed, "Oh, come on, Uta, sit down,"
she cried and slipped into a chair
as her companion just shook his head.

7

And now, as I pull words
into a form they might like,
now as I think of their eyes
and their built-in shrugs,
I wonder if we could ever sit
and tell the tales we've gathered
one by one for all these years,
wondering why and not caring.

We pull ourselves on to another day,
to something that might reassure,
that might help us understand
what the hell it's really about—
you know, the shuffling of pain,
the rewinding of our hopes.

8

And here we are on another island
where the hefty blondes laugh little
and our lunches at sea-food shacks
seem particularly enhanced
by clusters of them
who sit and tell each other
of empty nights when they knew
it was time to go.

Now here we are, I hear them say,
but there's no real laughter
in their eyes:
"I can hardly see," one said
the other day, "even the screen blurs
when I wake and try to turn it on."

9

Two of them sit at a table
where sun pours in
and the glitter from ice
in the parking lot
reflects on their glasses.
"It was never so pretty in Baltimore,"
one says in a voice that still purrs
like one of the demonic cats.

"But we were never out so early,"
the other says and reaches
for the sun, twists her fingers
as if to hold to the light and smiles:
"Besides, when were we ever…,"
she says and sighs, "at lunch by noon?"

10

I listen to hear if there is a sneer,
but they smile at each other
and look out at the light
until the deeper voice laughs.
"But don't you remember," she says,
"his name was Rufus
and he always came early
and afterwards wanted to eat."

"He wanted to go for a heavy lunch
of pancakes and ham."
They laugh again and even smile.
"God, I hated those breakfasts," one says;
"all I wanted was to go back to bed
and sleep without dreaming."

11

A lovely, aging friend,
with hair like snow that falls lightly
all afternoon, lost her graciousness
when I tried to tell her about
the whores we watch during our lunch
of raw oysters; she stared
for a moment or two and caught
her breath as she lost her smile.

"You don't understand," she said;
"this is a fine old town, full of churches
and help for the poor." Her son, on the other side
of the room, stretched out to stroke
his second wife. I know…: there are some things
one really shouldn't bring up in company.

12

"I can't let it go at that," she says,
pushing at the air that seems
to withdraw and leave her
with heavy breath. "Those days are gone.
I've been away from them for years.
It's not often we can take our masks
and throw them
into some far corner of the room."

It's rare and becomes rarer,
as it does to hold on to an afternoon
when we wander through corners
of the room and, behind the couch,
find masks. "I'm better now," she says
and adjusts her mask to a smile.

13

Will we ever understand?
You or I or those aging women I watch?
Perhaps, while sleeping away the afternoon,
I'll one day suddenly sit up
with that startled 'Of course!'
as I did once, a few weeks ago,
and knew I had the answer, knew
that finally, after all these years, I did.

I found what we crazy humans are all about;
and so, smiling to myself, almost laughing
with relief, fell back asleep
with heavy soundness; but when, an hour later,
I woke, I couldn't remember the answer;
I had forgotten once more and was left wondering.

14

I shall continue, now, and listen for clues;
I shall strain and hope my hearing holds
to all those possibilities that aging ladies
will drop over a salad and grilled cheese.
Surely if anyone knows what great philosophers
could never quite sort out,
it's the ex-whores of Ocean City,
especially the ones who can still smile.

And there are those rare occasions
when they look out across the room
and meet my eye and know I've been watching,
trying to hear, trying to figure out
what they've probably known for years,
just an answer to take away the question.

A WALK THROUGH A CEMETERY

It isn't death that worries me;
it never has been that.
I wake in the middle of the night
and remember with a smile a slow walk
through a Parisian cemetery,
for an hour or so in winter sun
that threw warm shivers down my spine—
or, years later, a slow boat trip
out to a Venetian island where the dead
seemed to invite us to settle
with camera or notebook,
and an old priest paused to exchange
a laugh or two about the silliness
of carvings that had fallen from the graves.

Not even the death of my father brought tears.
It was time; he had lived long
and whatever disagreements we'd had
are buried in complexities of memory
built like a rather beautiful Mondrian.
We took him to the grave
and watched unknown people try to look solemn;
and as we drove away, we laughed
and told funny stories he never liked.
Nor were there tears when mother died.
She forced a smile and went to bed
for a final time, never again,
I'm told, to open her eyes.
Death was a welcomed release.

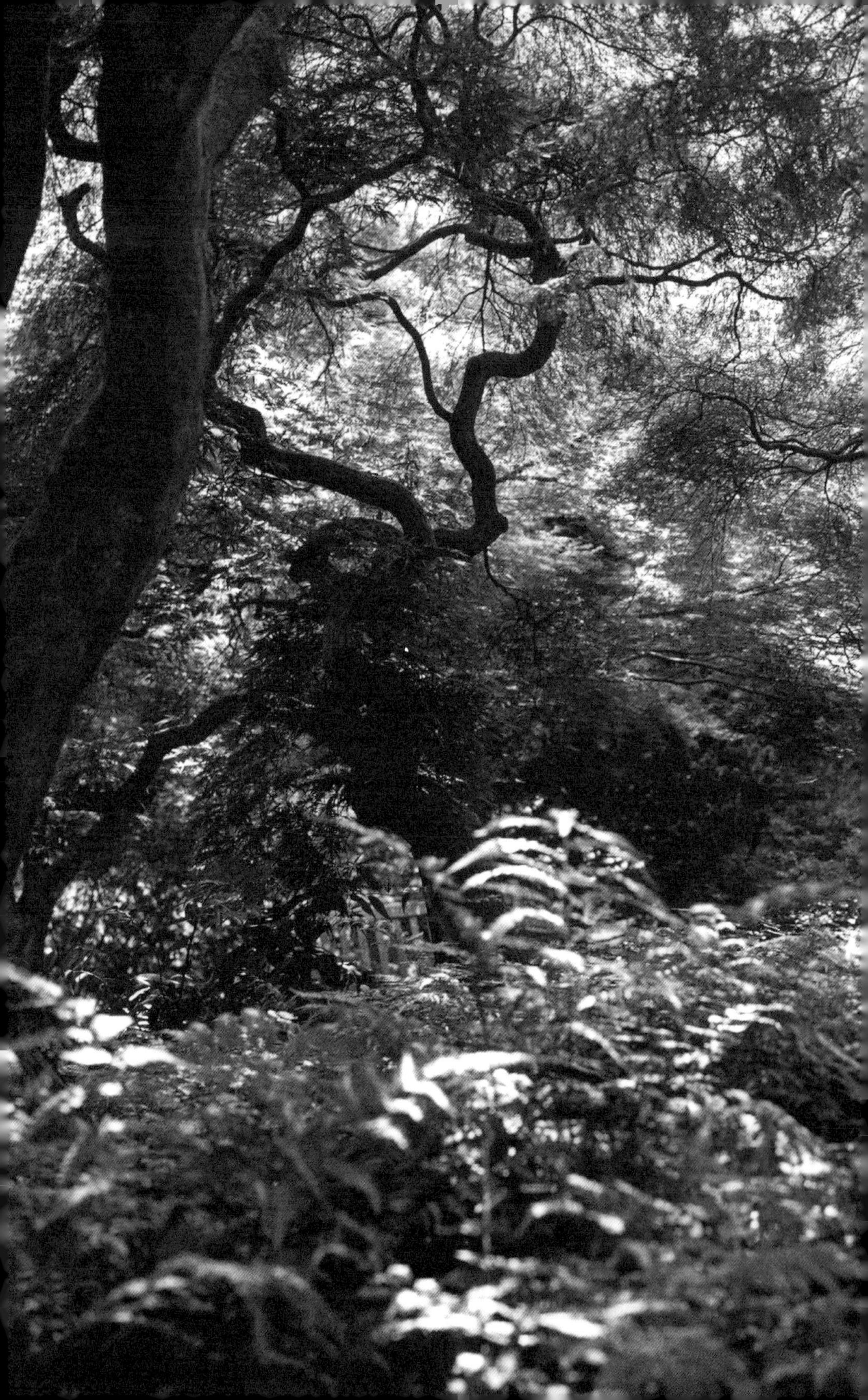

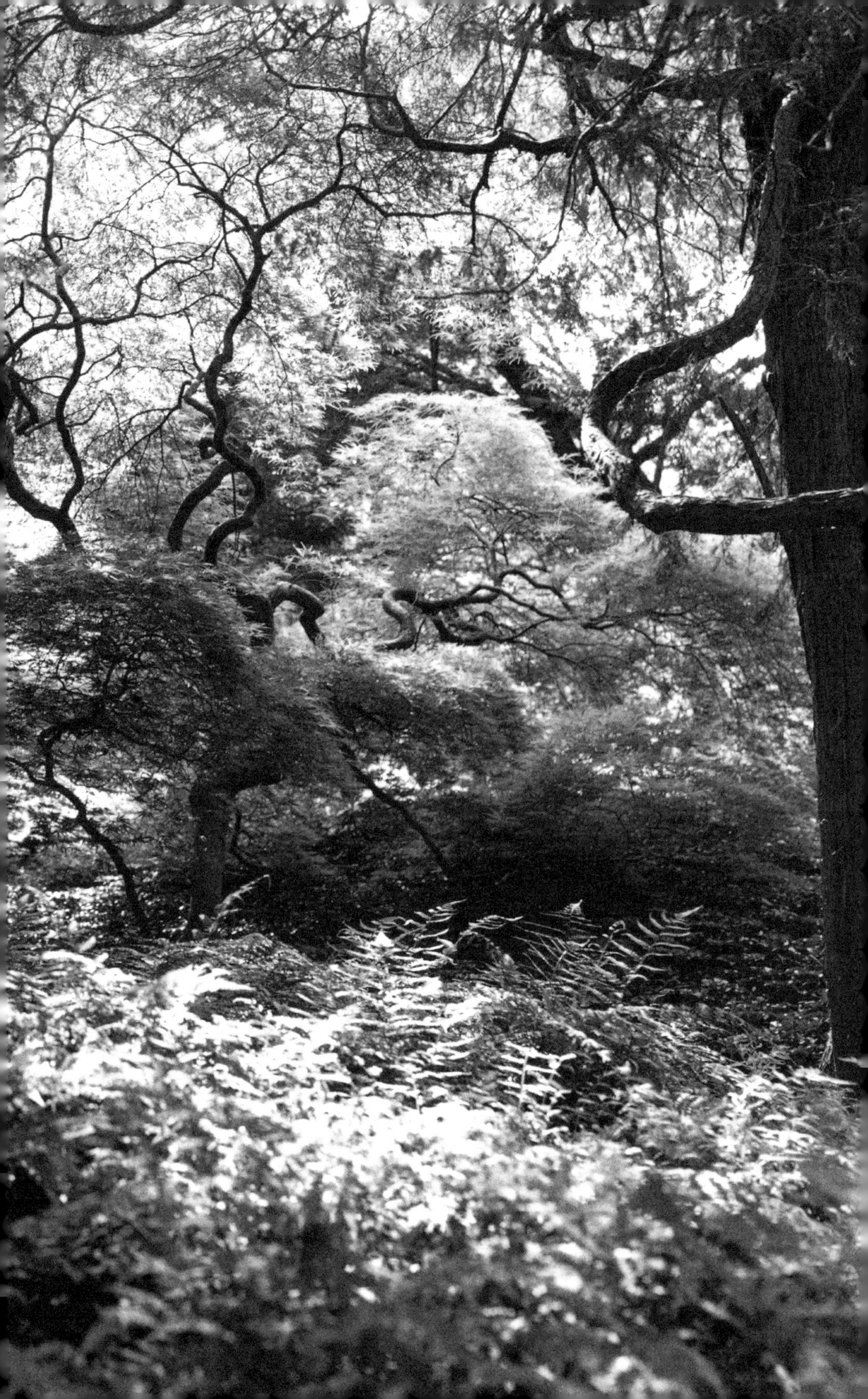

LATE PARTY

Dare I really say what I think of her,
or would that be like farting in a public place?
She used to grin and throw a curse across the room,
for there was, she said, no other way to pull it off;
and, sure enough, the room would shake
with awkward laughter, a sneeze,
a messy clearing of the throat; and the crowd
around the table of hors d'oeuvres
would thin and the hostess would rush out
with a fresh tray of frog legs and biscuits;
and then it was she who laughed, who flared
her eyes and looked across the table at me
and tried to catch my eye with a cast
into the deeper part of the evening
where fiddlers hid among stoned echoes.

That was a different time in this community,
when more of us seemed younger and bitter,
indifferent to what the blue-haired ladies
might think; and she and I competed
in our contempt for the proprieties of time
when latecomers would finish off the table
and she would pull back her line
with only a crab or two twitching at the hook;
until somewhere in the middle of the night,
she'd disappear and I'd wander the rooms
and find that almost everyone was gone
except for one or two at the kitchen table;
and with a last brief sniff of gin, I'd try
to chant the dirty song I had been humming
all evening as I followed her around.

QUESTION AND NO ANSWER

What's the answer when there's been no question?
It's like we're in a scene where all the dancers
disappear and the stage is left empty,
and we wonder if it's time to cheer;
but everything is still, the backstage empty,
and I stumble up the aisle and out the door,
wondering where she is, if she is there,
if, in fact, she even exists at all.

So, I ask again, what's the answer? You said
you had a question that only I could answer;
but, unfortunately, I've lost the answer,
have no idea what part of the verbal pile
might give an answer, or comfort a lack of knowing.
The theatre is empty now, the lights are off,
not even a rat bumps about the stage,
reminding us that, yes, she gave the answer.

I had sat until the dancers disappeared
and listened for a narrative that should
have helped me find just what the question is;
and now I'm lost down a dark alley
like those that use to tie the left banks of Paris
into a place where insecure young ones
could wander down unlit extensions of a stage,
and wonder if that was she just ahead.

I was 22 and that's been 58 years;
and if the dark alleys are no longer dark,
at least for me, canals are dark, and we pause
without knowing just what the sounds might be
when we pause and whisper to each other,
"Have you found the answer?" For years we search,
but she never arrives again, and the answers wait
as they always have without knowing the question.

BLACK BOTTLE OF WORDS

I

Recently an old friend wrote and, in a letter
or in my imagination, tried to remind me
what we had done as teenagers and tried to forget,
something to do with a big flawed football
player whose weakness we recognized,
perhaps when, back then as kids, we saw more
than we've recognized since—only, back then,
we didn't know, didn't yet have words to know.

I still don't know and never have known
what words are for what it's really like to *fit in;*
assuming that had I learned to laugh more,
I might have learned to fit in more;
in fact, though she has reminded me on occasion,
I still don't know whom she loved back then,
though we remember many things and laugh
and flirt now with stumbling impossibilities.

At least this is some of what's in a poem:
for poetry is music and, like field-holler blues
or even variations of Bach, means little
until performed with heart and head,
as I'm trying to do now about a friend
who tongued a phallic clarinet with teenage hope
of watching a stripper strip and couldn't,
in the process, even manage to keep a hard on.

Don't worry: I have been down in pines
really trying to listen to folk blues and jazz,
so now know why I don't enjoy Pine Top Perkins
and do love the guitar of Tom McManus;
so perhaps I should mention what friends and I
have often talked about over the last years,
that so much of what we make is metaphoric,
even when I am, really, listening to this jazz.

2

The reason why a black bottle in a painting
can be thrown far beyond the liquor cabinet
is because it is a metaphor: even the color
and texture of paint and ground are metaphoric;
certainly the hint or echo of something else
in the paint of the area surrounding the bottle
is metaphoric, as in a poem about that teen musician
split between demands of jazz and hunger for sex.

I often do not know what the metaphor literally is,
for it changes from day to day, even when words
do not change, except in the way in which they sway,
shifting their form, as a group of dancers,
as his painting of the 'Black Bottle' keeps changing,
for weeks changing as the painter works,
though I couldn't begin to find the words
to say what the literal metaphor was or is.

I wonder if the painter could tell me what it *means*,
or if the reader could: that it's black is important;
black is a major metaphor, as is wet or cold,
harsh or smooth, as is the clarinet,
as was that big football player, who had,
I now remember, only one arm, which makes
me wonder if that, the image of that one arm,
turns him into some special metaphor.

If I were a dancer, movement toward another
or away could be metaphoric, for sex attracts
or sex drives away, as words attract or drive away,
forming metaphors in even small clusters
of words or gobs of paint with shadows
that end up hanging on a wall or filling
the pages of a book and leave me wondering
if that black bottle carries dark nothingness.

SUBJECT MATTER

How do I know what the subject might be
before the subject has manifested itself
into a set of sentences with accurate syntax?
See, here, almost finished with a fourth line,
and I still can't tell Kira's ma the subject
I shall reach for here, somewhere between
the week I prefer not to celebrate
and the holiday that sneaks up day by day
as I try to find a polite way to write of retired
ladies from dancing clubs of Ocean City.

So, even as the sun slips to the horizon
on a cold day that started with storm clouds,
there are a thousand subjects waiting
for some of us to say something about.
Though I can't think of the subject to explore
with a cockeyed sentence that will make
a trooper of such wonderful people
as Kira's ma or even Kira or her pa,
before we dress and head inland to a farm
where goats will welcome us at the door.

BRASS POEM

I never thought I'd find a poem
that would fit so nicely, in its brassness,
on one of my collection shelves;
but then, suddenly, here was one
at the front door that I had failed
to answer when the doorbell rang
because I was too ill to receive her
and wondered how she knew I could use
another container for sweet smells
that make the smell of brass disappear.

I often pause before shelves of books
where brass objects linger and glitter
and reach up and pull a bowl down
and there's a moment when it carries
the sweet odor of rotting books,
for they do rot, especially those
that have lingered in old libraries
and fed whole colonies of worms,
as a friend said who said she'd leave
a poem that would be a bit different.

I've often sent a poem to one friend
or another; and many friends have sent
me one, sometimes something casual,
sometimes a rhythmic masterpiece
that I wish had been written by me;
but when the poem turns out to be
a piece of brass, something from China
that burnt hours of incense on a stove
and kept the air fresh, then I chuckle
to have such a thoroughly brassy friend.

WONDER OF WINDS

1

There are times when I hear the falling of water
in competition with a rustle of leaves, the snap
of palm fronds, and the call of an angry bird
unseen but somewhere out there in the brush—
they hold back the wind that tries to push
rising water into the very space where,
if dry, I'd stroll and dip to catch a large crab
or in a breathless dodge from a water snake
that, I'm told, isn't dangerous though his swish
reduces my breath and drives me back
to a raised deck where, as darkness falls,
we sit, each with a glass of wine, and perhaps read
a next page or two of a travel book that takes us
further even than this reach of water and wind.

2

My windows creak in the night and slam
against a structure about which I'm never sure,
like the sudden rise of a voice in a gym class
that drove me into quieter paths at the lake,
even at night when I knew gators would wait
for some feral cat or puppy abandoned
by the bitch who dropped them regularly,
though I was forbidden to bring one home,
or if I did, as once I did, a window was slammed
and I was told to sleep on the back porch
where wind hissed and sprayed all night,
popping the screen and making me believe
that I was abandoned, left on a desert
somewhere on the far side of the world.

3

A friend's voice sighs like wind among pines
when he calls to say he is caught in the undertow
and needs someone to pull him
from quicksand that caught him unawares
and left him waiting for her, though she never
appeared again, never called, left him there,
sinking, he says, sinking as wind pushes
water higher and higher, though how, I wonder,
can he hold the telephone up and out
of the neat denim shirt he always wears, strutting
between harassment of time and his own assurance
that, yes, he has it all—it is his;
and I would like to say I knew it could happen,
that winds could push us all to the quicksands.

4

The winds died around noon today, the hiss of water
dies, and now the whole house is quiet;
windows no longer beat a rhythm against the frame;
and I sit quietly just beyond the edge of despair
and think of all the friends who didn't make it,
who made one last call and then drifted into silence,
silence that can never exist with the winds,
insistent as they are, as full of reminders as they are;
and this silence reminds me that I have no memory
of silence as a child, for that memory is full of wind,
of hurricanes taking down palm trees, of a house
vibrating as I waited at the window and watched
the drama that could have carried us away,
and didn't, but left me full of sound that could.

ALPHABATTERY OF FRIENDS

Arguments are what we thrive on,
Regardless of results that leave us
Lingering in shadows,
Engulfing us in regrets or hopes, and like
Nothing else could
Enrich us beyond expectation.

Last time we had an argument,
One that sounded real at any rate,
Votive candles blew out,
Ending romantic possibilities.

are you forever defending yourselves,
not in an angry way, necessarily, but still
disjointed or otherwise?

Let's decide we love possibilities
Enriched by dreams or arguments,
Empty of antagonisms that drown the world.

Listen, my friends, let's keep it up,
Imbibing a fresh argument as if it were
Primed with herbs and glazes
Primarily used to enrich us with
More differences that we can enjoy
As they push us to the far edge of day where
Night will keep us, as it should, enriched.

TO HEAR HER

To hear her now, after all these years without a name
I'd recognize, without the voice that used to tease
whenever I stood up to read a poem in class;
and for a moment, now, I do not remember the tub
in which we spent afternoons while our mothers laughed
and pretended their marriages were going fine.

I listen for rhythms the autumn crickets make,
the beat they put upon the air when dark has fallen
and cicadas close down and from somewhere frogs
produce a deep underbeat, as if it were almost not there
in a trio Philip Glass never got around to drafting,
in an ensemble we might have played in school.

We played not because we played so well together,
but because we knew that no one else would know
what it was we were trying to bring together—
it would just be something they thought existed
among an elder few, not those of us who were
expected to play a little Mozart and bow and leave.

And was that really her in the tub without a stitch?
And did we ever touch with curiosity,
so that a mom would murmur, "Not there, my dear"?
Memory of childhood flushes with confusion
after almost eighty years and I rediscover her,
the lovely one who had good reason to tease.

VERBAL COINS

I

I do not know what it is I would say to you
        if I had the words,
if I had built a full-blown character of time
        from a casual pulse
when time was a great hall being structured
        further up river
where waters fell from a mountain
        across the afternoon
and I wandered freely
        through unfurnished corridors
and up the tidal falls until I couldn't
        find another way to go
and had to slip down in another direction,
        an unbalanced way
where I paused to catch my breath,
        and make certain
I was far enough from the edge
        to keep from falling
and wished that I could find words
        that would go wandering
through entirely different directions
        beyond my knowledge,
with gusts of wind between one cliff
        and another,
an imbalanced dance limited to a child
        of dreams who did not know
the hall would crash in a storm,
        and that no counting of time
could ever bring us through variations
        to assurance of a final cadence.

II

See, you've done it too, with a letter
          that stretches to become a poem;
and in places is verse, not prose,
          as often, when you, full of emotion,
use verse to avoid the curse that seems
          to teeter to the edge;
for that's when talk becomes the grand play
          it can be; we both know
that when we toss that verbal coin, as I do now,
          at this very moment,
when I try to keep the I-You riding for you
          through a part of the afternoon,
trying to give you a letter in response
          to the wonder you sent,
even if late, even if I don't have the energy
          to curry words like these
that, in order to become more of a poem,
          will break their form
and rattle across the page like ones
          I've spent a lifetime playing with;
for I really mean, how could I not respond
          with verbal energy to what you wrote
when, even in old age, words rise
          with phallic entheomania,
beset by the shape of phrases
          instead of the shape
of that blonde girl who was never interested;
          for remember, my friend,
that I am many years older than you,
          and that's pretty damned old.

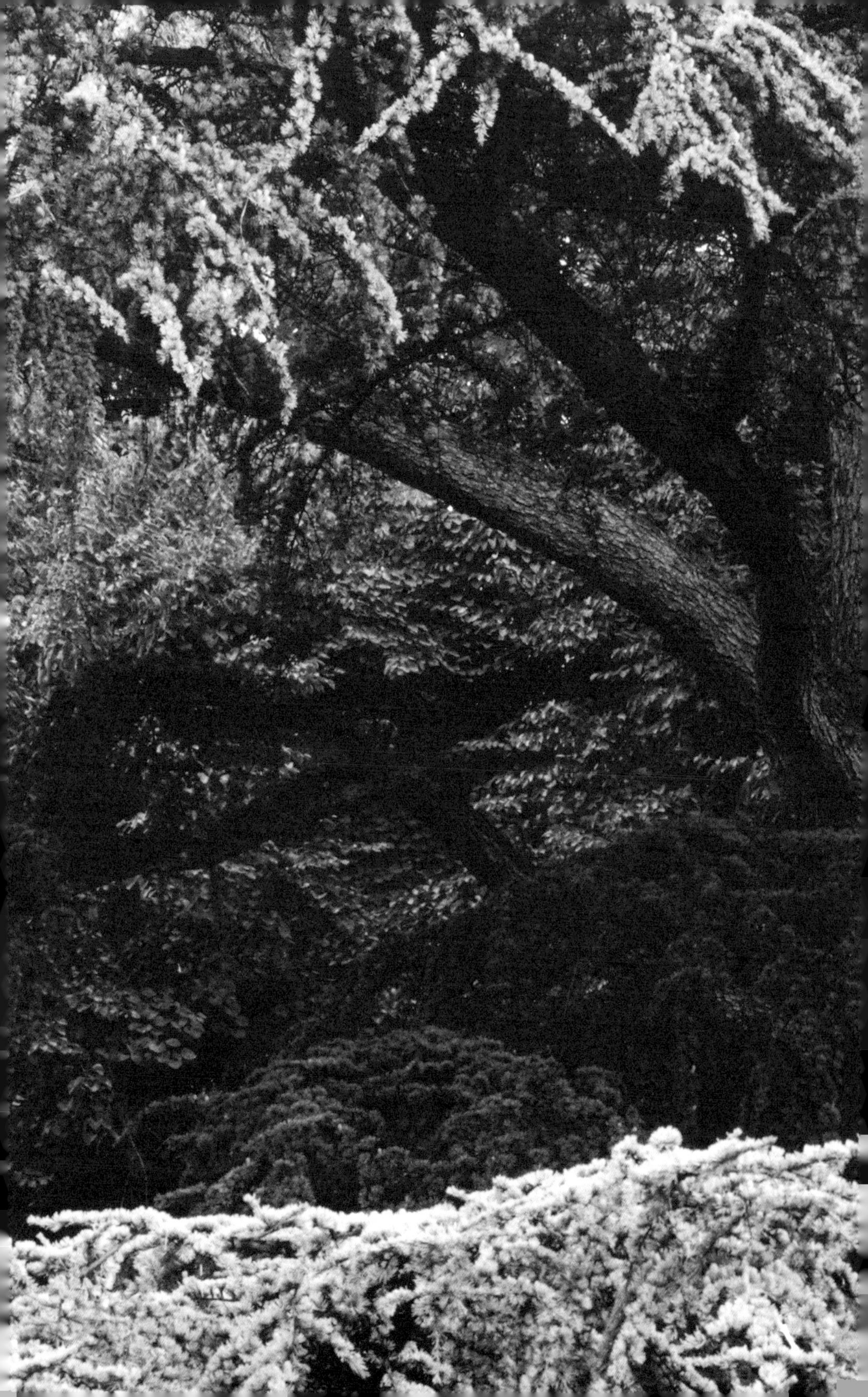

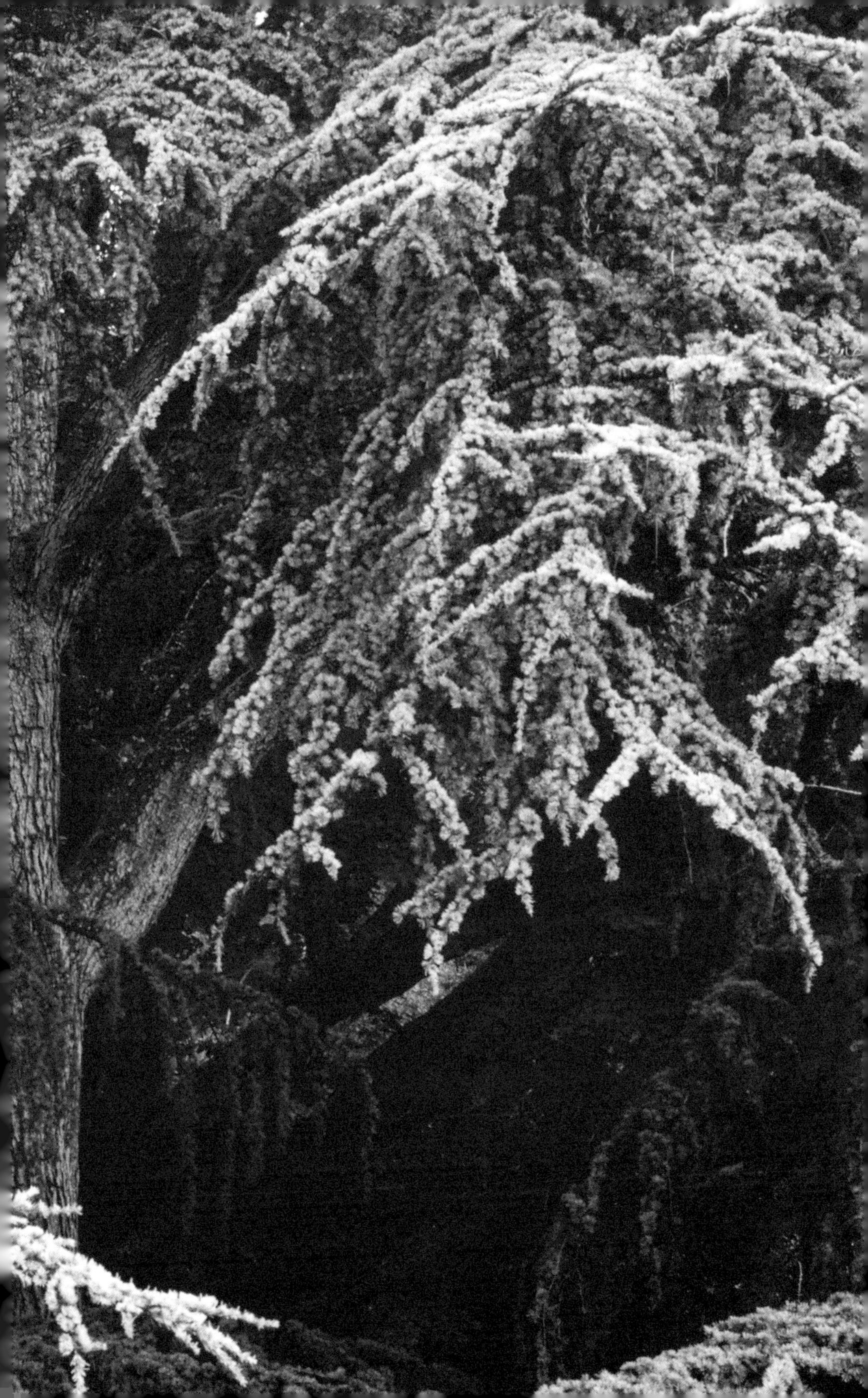

TOO SOON TO QUIT

I

No, no; not now—I can't quit now, not now;
there's so much more to do; I've just begun:
and there are piano concerti I've not yet heard,
and I'd like to understand the madness of Schumann
before I slip down the slope and find that's it.
No, no; not now: I haven't written that series
of poems that dance somewhere in my head.

I know I have to start them soon, before
the last day; and I have, I've started them
a hundred times and every time they go
another way and call a dozen to follow.
They're fine; I'm pleased with where they end;
but there are others that linger inside
with a syllable that bumps another syllable.

I've not even made one line or two, a stanza,
something to tell me that it could progress
and become a song to bring a tear to a friend
who tries to keep tears away from his eye,
who tries to tell me to turn away, avoid
the effort I've made to tell him how much I love
the relationship we could have had, if only….

If only what? It never worked, not then,
not now, as age tries to build a restless pile
that snuffles the air between just what we are
and what we could have been if only…. What?
Is this the poem for which I wait, for which
I drop a line; or is this like so much else,
another cluster from the words of Buber?

2

He knows what it is I try to say, this friend
who's found himself closed out from love
and left on a parking lot where cylinders leak;
and those who don't give a damn are still there
with angry tonalities on the telephone.
Yes, I'd like to read Leopardi with him,
in Italian without translations pushing my ear.

I'd like to say, "Now, Steve, let's get it together…."
How much time is there still left for us to find
what might let words flow free on afternoons
when there's intrusion from the stumbling body?
And so I sit here at the desk and watch
the sun as it creeps across the floor and stacks
of books that still are waiting to be read.

It's much too late, I know, to think this poem
might be the one I must write one day;
it has changed and swung off in another direction,
which is probably where it was headed anyway
as I felt around on a winter's sunny day
and thought of him who can't respond to love,
who may be dead before we share this poem.

Just another possibility of song,
another possibility of turbescence.
No, I have to tell myself, it's too soon:
I'd like to find how Bach managed to survive
so many children born and quickly dead
and still could leave such treasures lingering
when I've not yet played but a few of them.

3

At least I've put him in another poem,
and found a different set of words to use
before the opera starts as it did last week
so that the poem may have just what I want
and become a lovely thing that might bring tears
to another pair of friends who skirt the edge
as they paint, carve, and hope to find themselves.

They know it's there, right there, waiting for them
to recognize and place beneath the lights.
Meanwhile, I share whatever it is these words
will form on the afternoon screen, if not
what I thought of as I passed a pile of books
on the turn of the stair and couldn't remember
whatever it was I had wanted to achieve.

And what will come now? What will follow
while there is time before I am forced to quit?
In the middle of this poem, I heard an opera
I'd never heard, an early Verdi, *Attila,*
which gave me one less thing I have to know;
and earlier today a friend called to say
she'd be happy to teach me piano blues.

I've done a lot of reading recently
which makes it difficult to know the truth
of what really qualifies as the blues.
And while I ate my lunch, I thought again
of Steve somewhere among unhappy rooms
wondering if he sometimes thinks of me
and wishes we had shared more of our lives.

4

It's later now and the sun no longer falls
across these books on the deep window sill;
and there above the house the sky is clear
though pale, and more streaks of snow have melted;
and I wish I had the courage to call my friend
and ask if he is filling the void that opens
in all of us, a little more each year.

And I wonder if he has read a new poet
and rejoiced, or heard that piece by Samuel Barber,
as I just did, and wonder why it's now, just now
I've heard it with pleasure and wondered
what else might come before I have to quit.
That's why I know I cannot quit. Not yet.
No, not yet, if ever, can I quit.

So even when I do not hear the voice
I'd like to hear, even if it drags,
I'll remember to hear it in my heart, like Bach
when I open the pages I can no longer play
but can imagine, can close my eyes and hear
or see a painting I only know from a book.
No, that emptiness can still be added to.

We may have once held a great deal more
and may have thought as we reached the end
there would be no room for adding to the pile,
no room for listening to an old guitar,
unless the one we've known for seventy years;
but no, there's so much still to know, to hold,
to hear in the empty places of who we are.

TALKING WITH GULLS

I never thought that I would sit in a car
above the dunes of a bright ocean and watch,
without approach, a crash of waves just there,
clear as the center of atonal music,
draw back the sibilants of tide pursued
by gulls, two of whom remain beside the car
looking up at the window as if expecting
a scatter of crumbs to follow the voice I drop
in a private, silly moment, to warn the small,
black-headed creatures to be cautious as larger
white-headed ones approach with ugly intentions
in the raucous call of their awkward dives.

I've spent a lifetime wandering edges of the sea,
watching, from the deck of a house, barracuda
drive fry into leaps of panic and splashes;
or wandering to the end of awkward islands
not yet inundated with trailing human regrets;
or floating out to where a palm, the last,
lingers on a pebble of land above dead fish;
and never did it occur to me that time
might leave me lingering in an automobile
where I would talk to a silly gull and sigh
with rhythms of the sea, unable to reach down
and pull a shell from a chill of spring tides.

But here I was for an hour this afternoon,
while Andrea headed through dunes of sand
where remnants of turtles stank in falling sun,
and, from the car, I watched her face as it lifted
against the spray; and those impossible gulls
were back and forth against the wind, or just
below my window, and I started to wonder
if I could put them in a poem, in a clutch
of words where they might last a little longer
than I; so here they are, somewhere among
these words, somewhere among these memories
of a lovely afternoon, in spite of pain and age.

OLD TIN BOX

This old tin box, I am convinced,
since you sent it just yesterday,
is the burial box for a monstrous cousin
with whom I was terrifyingly familiar.
I am convinced at the same time
that this is the first time I've seen it
with my cousin's smashed face on it,
the face of an American athletic failure;
though this could be the tin he kept
his snuff in, for south Georgia crackers,
often crumbly, chewed snuff,
and spat the spit from the car window.

I love the conflict between negation
by all that black of silver and gold
and red and green and what seems
to come alive with cruel laughter.
It's what we had in old days:
no laughter without heavy darkness;
and then, within the tin box,
still dominated or rather swallowed
by black nothingness, these paintings,
these wonderful faces of three women
who, full of beauty, ache with pain
inflicted by indifferent men.

I don't remember these faces as aunts,
but do remember that sort of pain
in many of your paintings from then,
when all that was left was rotten red fruit,
not in the painting but jammed in a barn
with stuff where I suddenly saw a piece
of old wood, not unlike the slab
on which you rest your final fruit
where a feral cat and kittens were
dead in the hollow of an apple tree
that has since blown down and left
remains of final fruit in black distress.

WHERE DO WE GO

1

Where then do we go from here? she said.
In what direction? Shall I head for the sun
that sets across the bay, or back
where morning begins another day
when we'll not know just what direction
we'll find ourselves in before dark
falls again? Shall I try now to decide
if we'll arrive where we know
we can remain and even settle in
and breathe with a little more attention
to the rhythmic beats that keep the body
moving like a line of verse?
But where, she says again, do we stop—
where will cadence close and let us be?

2

No easy question for either of us
to drop beside the other's plate;
no easy question to whisper at night
when sleep keeps struggling with the day;
and certainly these are not the questions
that either of us would argue over.
They don't ask for such intensity;
they're just the kind of question a painter
might ask as her brush pulls across
with one color and pauses to wonder
if another color might do as well
with a touch of yellow streaking the sky
she thought would linger in the grays
but now demands a little more.

3

This afternoon an old friend called
while I was wondering why the Bach
was different, why it seemed to slide
away from the cello I listened to
when Andrea was in some other direction.
"It's I," he said, "why haven't you called.
We're almost ready to hit our eighties;
we've got to find just where we'll go
as nights get longer. You remember,"
he said, "it's been at least three decades.
We said we'd reach before the dark
slipped over the grays we knew would come."
A little streak of yellow, I thought,
that's all that's left before the end.

4

I could only remember he lived in a house
that washed away, as so many things
were blown away with the bombs of the day;
and we were looking for a way to go,
which wasn't with another, yet.
For him it never would be; for me,
well, I was lucky, I found another
who was not afraid to ask, "Where now?"
And then she'd try a mountain top
with an echo in a Buddhist temple
like a splash of gold across the quest
that's closer now to a final dark
falling from one direction or another,
with a little hope in that streak of gold.

UNDERSTANDING

I wonder why and have never known why
and wonder now if I will ever know,
if you could tell me in some simple words,
if you could drop a hint or two in words
that might just splat across the table where books
are piled that never seem to give an answer,
even if bright with paintings of the Buddha
and his smile that breaks across the room at night
and caused a priest with very little English
to fall across the rug and spill a chant
with apologies that none could understand,
not even you, or so I seem to remember,
as you dropped a smile and said you understood
it was an answer that drifted without words.

So why is it only now I push at you
to tell me what the answer is, to bring
me close to a time when I and you will know,
when both of us can settle in to last books,
to those we've said for years we had to read
before another stratification came
that might just leave us in the storage bins
I've spent a lifetime cramming with the past—
and now the bins are full. Do you remember?
We swore we'd never let that happen, no,
not us, for we would keep the words at a flow
of quietude like the sleeping Buddha stretched
beside the flute that waits in the music room,
that waits with sounds beyond a verbal power.

I look around at objects we have gathered,
ancient heads we found in a tropic sandbar,
bells that ring with pride of mountain gods,
paintings done by friends who've long been dead,
whose names I can't remember except that she
was unwilling to pull me close, had even forgot
to send me words that might relieve the pain
and remind me what we were meant to know
when all those years ago we flirted and laughed,
before you too had wandered away and left
the words I'd piled in notebooks still right here
beside the desk, fading now, as words
will fade if they're not used, like old brass pots
that monks held out for a bowl of rice and hope.

Yes, our words may disappear, slip down
behind a piano I can no longer play,
even if I punch a note or two of Bach
and find my hands pull up like forgotten words
I had hoped to share with you before the end.
Even if it was another argument
or that song we tried to sing before you left,
now we have to sigh and maybe drop
a tear, you know, the kind of tear that came
when words ran out and down the page and we,
yes you and I, decided it was better to hold
the words like sprinkles of laughter and tears,
for then we'd know that they had been for real
and might just echo until the very end.

EDGY FRIEND

If I were to write an account of an extremely gifted,
edgy, middle-aged male—and that was all I knew,
nothing else—what words would I use to begin the pile?
It is the middle of those three givens, *edgy,*
that makes for possibilities, which may be why,
though I nearly always put people within my poems,
I rarely write prose, which seems more natural for people.

If I do, the prose is a piece of personal memoir
featuring an aging and rather droopy singleton,
as I've just done in a poetic-prose piece called
"Looking Back Where Words Began." More likely,
of course (of course I can say *of course*), if *male*
wasn't one of the three, the piece might be one
of the sonnets I started last week about retired whores.

But wait a minute, none of this is what I set out
to write on an early Monday morning under a clear sky,
though with a thin unmarked yellow haze, at least
at the moment the sun came up through the pine forest.
What really pleased me, however, was the setting
of the full moon, at something after 6 this morning,
into the bay, just there where I could watch it.

Not quite, though I could if I lifted my head and found
my glasses—or was it when I got up for an early pee?
At any rate, I don't think I've ever seen
a full moon sink into the sea, though we've often lived
over waters that stretch to the west where I have seen
darting sharks and a thousand sinking suns; maybe
it takes a collision of chances to wake as the moon sets.

Damn, here I go again, forgetting the edgy friend
who would make a good subject for a pile of words
that might take the form of a quaker house his mother
had lived in so long ago I barely remember when we met,
when he and I, I think, were in the army training to be
secret agents, an activity his mother dismissed
when she showed me how creative doing a garden is.

To surround the house with gardens and trees would smooth
the edginess that weapons bring to midnight wakings.
Almost square the house was, white with black shutters,
as if that has anything to do with a portrait of her son,
if it was he I suddenly remembered when I started
this pile some weeks ago before I had decided
whom I had in mind—not this edgy friend or his mother.

It's not that I remember. Not at all. But just today
an e-mail arrived to say his wife, a painter who never
went beyond the soft abstractions she did as a student,
has died; and suddenly I think of what an edgy friend
he has been and wonder if that could complete this pile
that has for weeks seemed scattered. In fact, the poem
began when I was down among pine trees on the bay.

When I came back limping without a balance,
I decided perhaps it wasn't he, for there's another friend,
closer, who has dismissed me often during the last
thirty years, because, I think, I've not been able to help
him manipulate a way through thorns—those that
make a pile of words dangerous when you start
digging down through them to find your heart.

LACK OF KNOWING

1

So little I know, so much to know;
like why clouds, not seen all day, suddenly rise
as if in anger from a sky brilliantly clear
as the sun sets and seem to split the crescent
with scratches a Chinese scholar might make —
and the sun starts slowly to flatten and slips
silently behind a distant line of the bay,
over there, beyond NASA, somewhere
out there in a world I do not know,
out there beyond a world I can only imagine —
while here, with a bottle of wine, we wait
in silence, not touching, just waiting
as we watch the sun widen until it narrows
and with a flash of green slips away.

2

I sit and feel the paint flake from
the structural edges of this old body,
where windows are so cracked and dirty
that I can hardly see what's out there,
not from here, at any rate, where I wait
for wind to rise even more and the backbone
to shift as the sun falls and darkness settles
with a whir among us old pines that might
at any moment suddenly lift from the earth
our roots and slide over and down
among younger ones, pulling us
into a crash across the eaves
of an old house that no one seems to care
was ever here or crushed in the last storm.

3

Why, I ask myself, why do the good ones
linger in a fretful state above the cliff
where they have seen so much that could be known
and blown it into paintings for another day
when someone is likely to ask just what we knew,
anyway, us aging out-of-date mufflers
who thought we had something that might last
to be put together and left in a pile behind the garage
or in the attic of a journal we left with the world,
as if the world could care; yes, there are many
who tried, who put it down in clay or ink
or left it smeared across the top of an old desk,
who fret and restlessly struggle, here on the edge
of the cliff, to find again a box of fresh hopes.

4

Is there any way I can say I know?
I know I'll never finish the song
you started, yes, long ago—I heard
the tones shift as you edged closer
to what the day might bring.
And, yes, suddenly, do you remember?
we were caught by age and started the anger
and regrets that led us to wonder
if we would ever get it all together
into one pile, a set of organized rejoices.
Remember? The rejoice we said we'd seize
the moment it appeared, if ever it did;
and now I understand you've piled it all
in a rented shack just down the street.

DEATH OF A LIME TREE

I think I may go like the lime tree below
this window; it has wilted and sagged
and left its fruit irretrievably rotten.

It's inevitable what age can do
that creeps through cracking that comes
no matter what we thought might flourish.

Of course, this far from tropics, in frost,
a lime tree must be carried into silence
for the winter, or left on an isolated island.

You've been there, on the island
where we sniffed at limes and waited
to see what might survive, if not flourish.

ASH IN A FOUND POEM

When Georgia resident Raymond Detrich's house
was burglarized recently, thieves ignored a wide screen
plasma TV, a computer, and even left his Rolex watch.
What they did take, however, was a generic white

cardboard box filled with a grayish-white powder.
At least that's the way the police report described it.
The same report said it looked like high grade cocaine
and thieves probably thought they'd hit the big time.

Later, Detrich stood in front of numerous TV cameras
with tears in his eyes and pleaded with the burglars
to please return "the cremated remains of my wife,
Gertrude, who died just two years ago last week."

The next morning, the bullet-riddled corpse of a local
drug dealer known as Hoochie Prevens was found
on Detrich's doorstep. The cardboard box was there;
and about half of Gertrude's ashes remained.

Scotch-taped to the box was a note: "Hoochie
sold us the bogus blow, so we wasted Hoochie.
Sorry we snorted your wife.
No hard feelings. And have a nice day."

> *(An old friend sent me a version*
> *of this tale from a local paper.)*

GRAVEYARD WIND

Heavy winds blow gravestones, have blown
them for generations that now seem to be gone;
and someone at the local tavern says
that the family, one of the first on the island,
has disappeared and no one knows who was
the last to die, for names are faded or chipped
from stones that spend half the year in crud
as most of the fields flourish for a season
with corn or beans and gravestones disappear,
perhaps forgotten; though sometimes on a day,
sunny in spite of chills, we wander among stones
that seem to shift, too restless for unnamed bodies,
left only as dust if even that. No box, not even tin,
shows someone might have cared, surely someone
might remember the old lady who held on longer
than even the fallen house that leaves a rotting cluster
of trash on the edge of the field, a little less,
it seems, each time we pass and slow down to see
how many stones even if rubbed and almost blank,
remain as fields die down and a few more stones
recline, a few more disappear, perhaps to make
a path around a trailer just pulled to the edge
of the road, by one who never knew this family
was one left blown by endless wind,
was never cursed by the old lady who drove
curious wanderers away with a shout
from a crumbling window of the rotting shack
that crunched into the ground as she disappeared
and left the village indifferent to where she was.

MAKING NOTES

I woke at one and chanted a line of verse
and lay awake and thought, "That's not so bad;
in fact, it just might make a poem behave."
And then, this morning, early, unable to see
the clock, I forgot the line, could not remember
what I had failed to note on cards
I keep just there beneath a chilly pillow.

It was a good line, but it's gone and these
few lines are caught to tell me not to forget,
to make my notes as soon as they pop out,
not to let darkness of time linger,
bumping through tight corners of the room;
after all, it's that unexpected birth of words
that makes a poem reshelf itself with hope.

I've pulled a bunch of words from margins
of old books, ones I carried through pathways
of Switzerland and found, years later, high
on top of poetry shelves in dark nooks
and wished they had not lingered so long,
though at least they were scribbled with words
that, years later, found their way into songs.

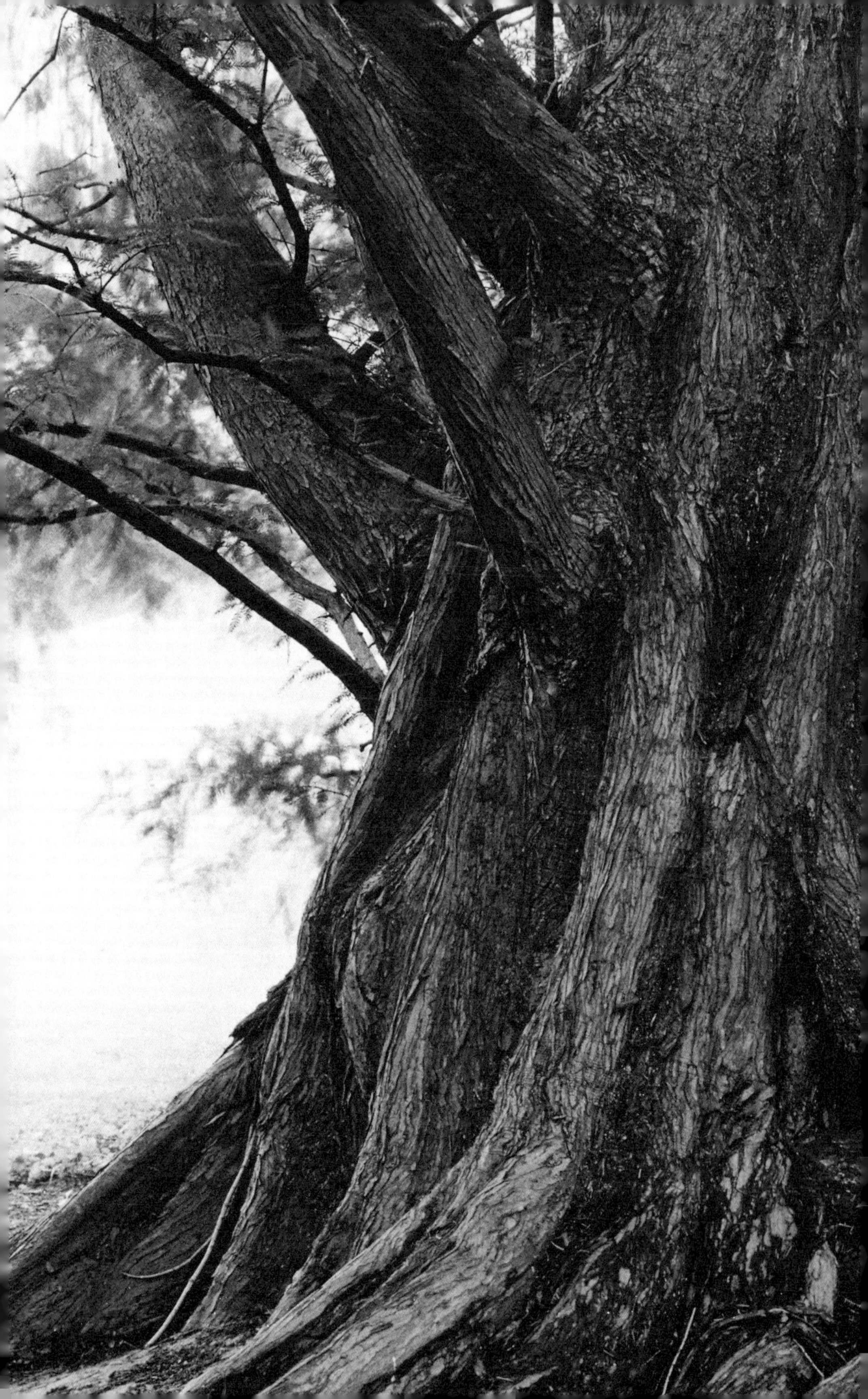

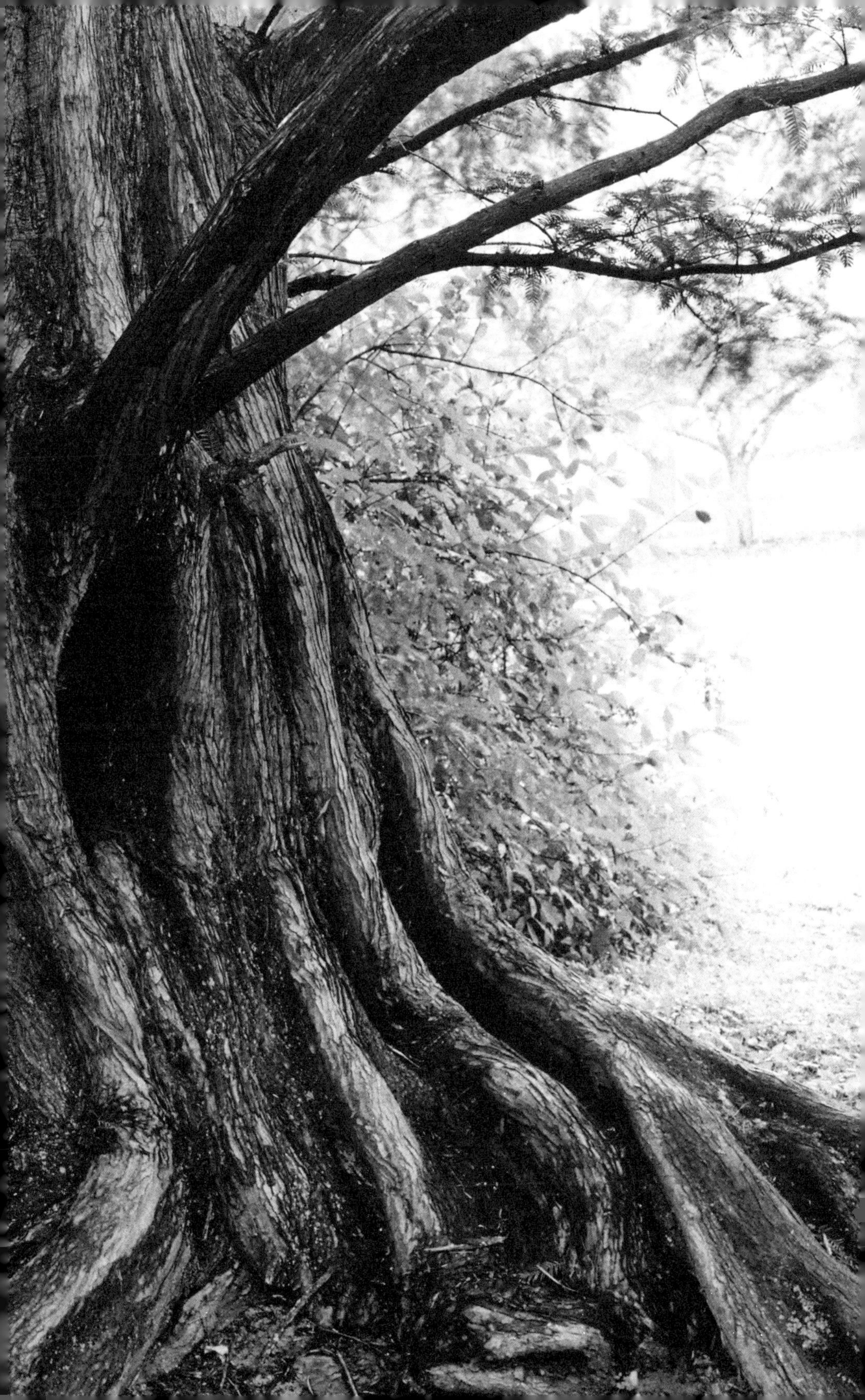

VOICES RIGHT HERE

Where is *there* if not here? Where were you
when voices spilled from somewhere here,
or over there, and we wondered from where
they may have come or from whom?

There was no one else around, not here,
the only place we would have known where;
not in spaces that stretch across the bay
or fall with wind from sweeping pine trees.

No; but there were voices that were more,
a tide rising through swamp grass that sways
with the energy of dancers who move across
the stage as if pushed by a drift of wind.

But dancers don't shout and whisper words
as the sun sets; and what I hear, somewhere,
are voices that urge us to…, something I can't
quite hear, but it's there, if not right here.

I hear it; I do. Don't you? Voices I think
I know, if I slow down and listen carefully;
see, right there, somewhere just behind me,
a lifetime of whispering hope or fear.

Are you afraid tonight, or is it I? Listen,
maybe these are the voices you brought to me
and left for me to use or follow through day,
voices that share a life of possibilities.

RESTLESSNESS

I wondered where I'd end up wandering
if all I did was wander through the night;
and there were times that happened every night:
I wandered away from dreams, pulled on a sweater,
and took an elevator to the quiet street,
not crowded as in the mornings or in my dreams,
but crowded with possibilities I couldn't
ignore, not then, at fifty, thinking that I
was on my own for whatever duration there was.

I wasn't out to make connections with blondes
or laughing drinkers in the corner bar.
Not then, not that; though I was never sure
just what I might be looking for—not then.
Perhaps it was whatever life threw shadows
within a brightly lit window high on the façade
of a house where there was no one that I knew—
it was just a window within which strangers moved,
perhaps with the same restlessness I felt.

Much younger then, I'd wander until the sky
would show release, relief from heavy dark,
and other windows would fill with early lights
and I'd return, but not to bed, not yet.
I'd go and sit in a window from which I'd watch
the city come alive, watch early workers
push on into the light as traffic thickened;
and then with light and turmoil of the day
I'd smile, relieved, and go to bed and sleep.

ONCE UPON A TIME

Once upon a time, a long time ago…,
is the way stories started, way back then,
when grandfather read them in a soft voice.
Afterwards, that was the world from which I rose;
though where, I wonder, is that world and why
is it I can't remember except as a chapter
where opens a book he read or was reading
at that very moment, right there beside the bed
in which, for too long, I spent my days —
where, for so long a time, I waited for him
to return from Georgia to read another
that began, of course, with *once upon a time.*

He taught me to repeat the reading, to begin
with *once upon a time;* and I did — that is
where I began even after he came
to the hospital window in Savannah
and waved farewell one last time, leaving me
to wonder why he never came again.

Still, I close my eyes and hear his voice,
and know for certain it is his voice that starts
once again, with *once upon a time.*
And even now when I am older than he
ever got to be, he's the ageless grandfather
inside my head, beside the bed, right here
with whispered reassurances that he
was there even when he stepped aside
for a long time to find another book
to read, to leave on the edge of memory,
and tell me what it was I'd find in all
that trailing dust of time from then to now.

LAST NOTES

If the last notes of the sonata I played this morning
failed to resolve themselves, could it have been
a twist that Mozart decided he had no choice but to give,
leaving a final cadence as something for us to regret?
It could have been because, at six, his only son died
and an incomplete phrase echoed a missing life.

But it was I who failed to find the final cadence:
my fingers, swollen and carrying the weight of age,
simply quit, could not continue in the game
to fill a room with flow and balance of sound
that I had manipulated, with occasional burrows,
during most stumbling years I'd managed to clear.

Of course there were slips, as in a Bach I thought I knew,
over which I stumbled during a luncheon for ladies
bound to know, who didn't wince but applauded,
much to my discomfort; though maybe that's what led
to more attention to where the notes were really
supposed to go, up there, then down, in resolution.

So now I'll have to think a little harder; perhaps
I'll move a little slower, just enough to bring a close
to a pattern that's ready to move on up the scale,
that's ready to find another way to keep going,
even when I wince at the pain to keep the search
going if only temporarily to a final cadence.

AN OLD MAN REMEMBERS SEX

I

Stumbly and tired, I pick up his collected poems
        and reread the Allen Ginsberg not read in decades,
shifting from page to page across years when he,
        a bit older than I, wrote much
and fucked odds and ends of minor poets I used to keep
        piled at the back of my desk;
it isn't that his description of finally fucking an old friend,
        pretty as a post card,
turned me on; it didn't and I don't think it ever would
        and that's what I think I miss—
not that I want or ever wanted to grab a male cock
        in my mouth and lick and chew;
though if I had, I wonder if I would have lasted longer
        in the delicious turmoil of phallic explosions,
especially if I were, even now, to reach down,
        between poems, and squeeze the limp cock;
but since I can't do that any more, I sit here
        with the poems of Allen Ginsberg and imagine
the piles of poems scattered about my office and wonder
        if I will ever get them all into print;
though I must admit it's a possibility that brings up
        all sorts of alternative problems,
especially as I sit here trying to write a poem
        that bows to the form I swiped from Ginsberg—
and I must admit that I had not remembered
        the sweeping beat of sex he used so freely
even back then when he was still so young,
        not an old man like me trying to remember sex.

II

Yes, that's it; that's what I'm trying to do now as I sit here
    and watch the fading of afternoon light;
trying to remember, trying to tell myself that, yes, even
    if it were another time, there were evenings
when the rhythms of the Gulf waters would make us
    hungry for a slow pressure against the body,
especially one of those bodies topped with blonde hair
    and a grin that made me wonder what it was
she was really trying to say—though I must say that I
    was never really sure except when she laughed
and said, "Come off it, you idiot, that's not where you
    and I are going;" and, maybe, just for a moment
our hands would drop across the other's body
    at the moment a large fish splashed in the surf
or a great bolt of lightning flashed across the sky
    right there where, moments before, we had watched
a large sun elongate itself and sink into the sea,
    sink right out there where we had floated
during the hotter part of the day and brushed one self
    against the other as someone called from the shore
and laughed, though now there was no one to laugh or call
    and the isolation was almost too much, frightening,
and I still wonder if there could have been more,
    if we might have reached a point of sudden shift,
a sudden release into stretching pleasure that now
    seems forever gone, slipped away,
beyond where even the full moon now gives dreams
    a lift through richness of the night.

BACH'S CELLO SUITES

I've listened to them for most of my life
and always assumed they were here to hear
whenever I may have started my life.
Yes, these cello suites that, apparently,
Bach left carelessly on the back porch
until they disappeared for 200 years
when a boy the age I was when I heard them
for the first time found them in a pile of books
and brought them to the light once more.

So when was it I first heard the rising
of those strings, the movement of sound
that said I was hearing something different,
I was hearing something that would carry me
somewhere else, somewhere I had never been?
That's possibly what I could have said
about those sonatas I played when I was 10;
but no, it isn't: I complained about repetitions
in Mozart's base in sonatas I now adore.

I could swear I heard a wandering cellist
play them at the local college before the war,
as I sat on the floor in a corner of the room
and wondered just where I was, forgot
that Professor Barnum had told me to come
and listen; and suddenly I knew I'd never
have to be told that again, not ever—this
was something I was born to hear,
though not to play, not for the piano.

Is that the great gap in my life, that I waited
until now to put those notes, even with
my aging awkwardness, onto piano keys?
And now, with darkness falling ever closer
to the evening of this life, I do not try
to be a cellist, I just pull the notes of Bach
deeper into my heart, deeper into the world
I've known and loved for almost 80 years,
deeper into that world to whom he gave life.

No, not even this is meant to be annihilation;
there are no regrets even here: for all along
I've heard the notes, I've felt the presence.
So wasn't that really a cello suite I heard
in a small recital room at Florida Southern?
Didn't even a small two-part *Invention*
carry the possibilities of a cello suite,
always here to hear, even before the notes
were printed and available again?

OLD ONES

1

We used to laugh when an old one's voice
would call from a park bench and tell us
to get out of there, to find another way home.
"This park ain't for you," one of them would yell;
and, yes, we'd laugh and run in circles
around their bench until one rose like a giant
and we'd drop laughter and head toward home.

Oh, but that was a long time ago and now
we're the old ones hanging out in the park,
waiting to frighten the kids who come
to laugh at us and our lingering slur on age;
or we would be, except there's no park bench
in the area where any of us now live, waiting,
and few children in the neighborhoods.

2

There seemed to be so many of them back then,
a table of old ones who often came for dinner
and talk while all us kids were sent to the kitchen
where we would listen through a swinging door,
trying to know just what it was the old ones
might say when the kids were away and they
were left to find their own way elsewhere.

Could it really have been as wild as we hoped?
It isn't today. There never seem to be young ones
either at the table or in the next room; and only
seldom are there others, growing old
and talking about a new young painter
at the gallery who seems to have lost touch
with the fleeting structure of the human body.

3

We used to watch all those who returned
from war with a cane and a limp, and waited
to hear what they might say about dead bodies
in a trench, all those who never returned;
and when they reached for a beer with a hand
that sometimes dropped a glass in a shatter
across the table, we did not laugh or run.

There always seemed to be a group of them,
from one war or another, sitting on a pier
and drinking beer and waiting for us to ask
just what it might have been all about
and if it was over now, if we might be a part
of the next one that came along, the next war,
the next obliteration of a generation.

4

It's different now. We know there will be
another—there's hardly a separation between one
and the next; and we'd just as soon not talk
to kids who'll soon be off on another glide
through one burning village or another.
In fact, we rarely see the young ones unless
we've spent our time in a classroom.

And where has the laughter gone? It has;
and now that almost everyone we knew is old,
we wonder if we had been the last to laugh,
to sit in a park that no longer exists and laugh
at old ones who occasionally frightened us
by being the only ones to fall asleep on a bench
and wake suddenly and rise and frighten the kids.

WILD HORSES DANCE TO *SWAN LAKE*

How inappropriate, I tell myself, to have
'Swan Lake', even if only Act II, playing
on the car radio as the local wild horses
bring themselves closer and closer, snuffing
and pausing to push once more against
their stallion, who, if anything, lets
his phallus hang loose and apparently
exhausted while the music of Tchaikovsky,
a favorite of mine 60 years ago,
seems as exhausted as he does, he who
may well know that the young ones,
just down the dunes, are waiting to see
which one will move in and take the herd,
leaving him scratched out by dying strings.

No, but again I was wrong, as so often:
not even the strings are ready to quit;
it's almost as if the dancers are still fecund,
still having fun, not yet ready to settle in,
ready for the kind of march up the shore
that young stallions take when suddenly
they decide to move back closer to the herd
their father had ruled for at least a decade,
like one of the great male dancers I watched
as he sweated alone on his last stage,
with no chorus, no beautiful cluster of mares,
alone with aging breathlessness, in spite
of a moment when movement across the dune
carried a brief remembrance of gracefulness.

FRIENDSHIP THAT FAILED

It isn't often I can say what I really think,
not when he's suddenly there again;
I look in his eye and see the boredom he feels;
his smile looks like an angry dog's dismissal.
So then I laugh and know it's as fake as his smile
and always has been, for the 40 years we've known
each other, the years we've tried to be friends
and failed. At least a dog will never live so long;
he'll simply disappear in the field above the house
and a few days later we'll find the body,
a bit rotten now and stinky, but there will be
that glare at the edge of an eye, that dismissal
that left me indifferent to pets around the house,
that left it difficult to tolerate the friendship
of a few people I've known and admired,
a few I've wanted to understand, wanted to love
beyond friendship that becomes difficult with age.

I really think we could have been real friends,
in spite of how he treated the world of others,
the way he pissed in the corners of our lives.
And yet, it's only his words that linger in memory,
only his words that remind me of what I saw,
for I haven't really seen him in several years;
and now his words fall apart with whatever
they were meant to say; they snarl and stumble
like an angry dog that doesn't understand
just what it is that stinks and disappears.
I guess it all does that, disappears before
we know just what it is really all about.
He's a friend who should have been, who kicked
at the open door and darted out for a run
through the world, for something I never
understood as I looked him in the eye and tried
to know whatever it was that lingered there.

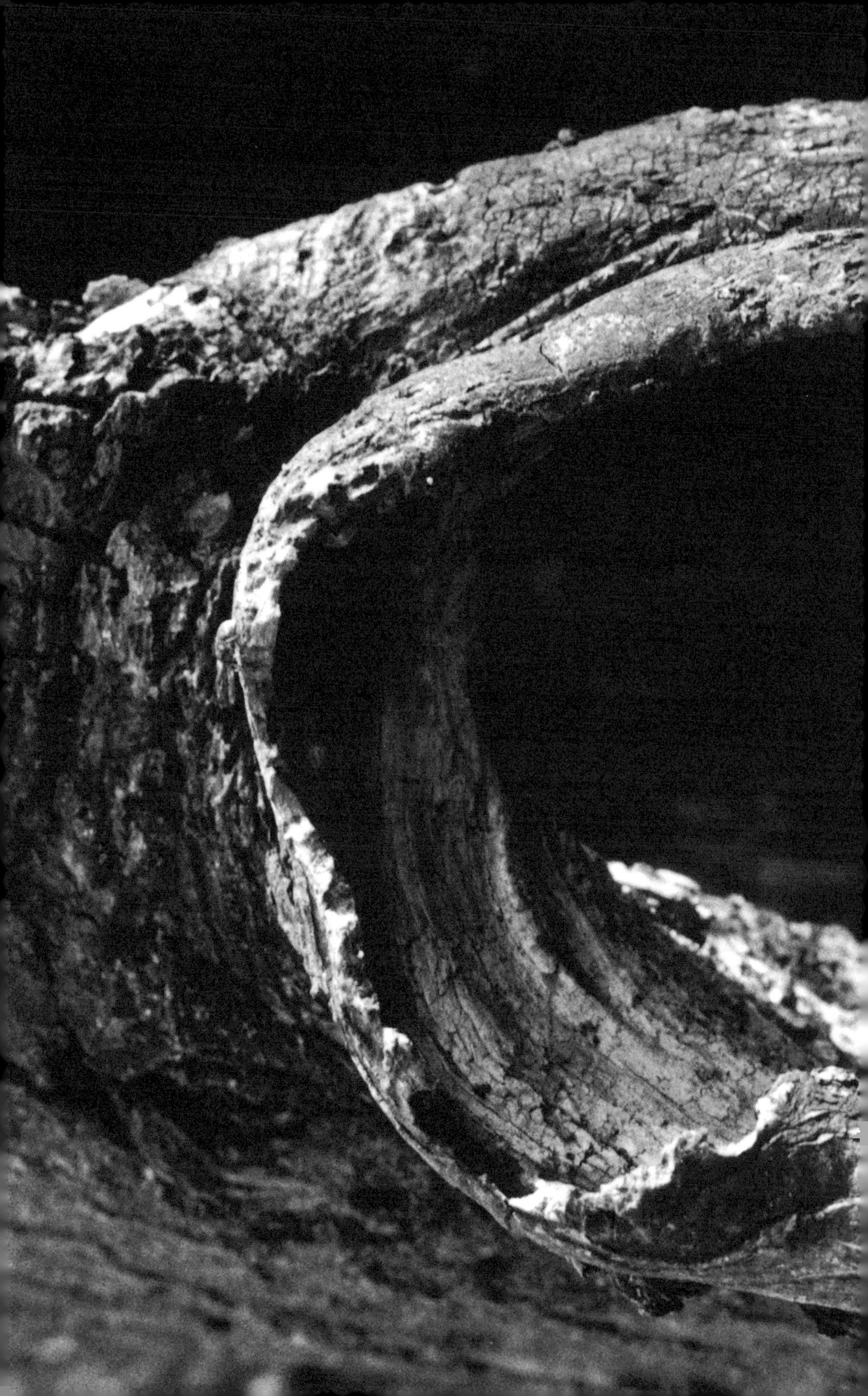

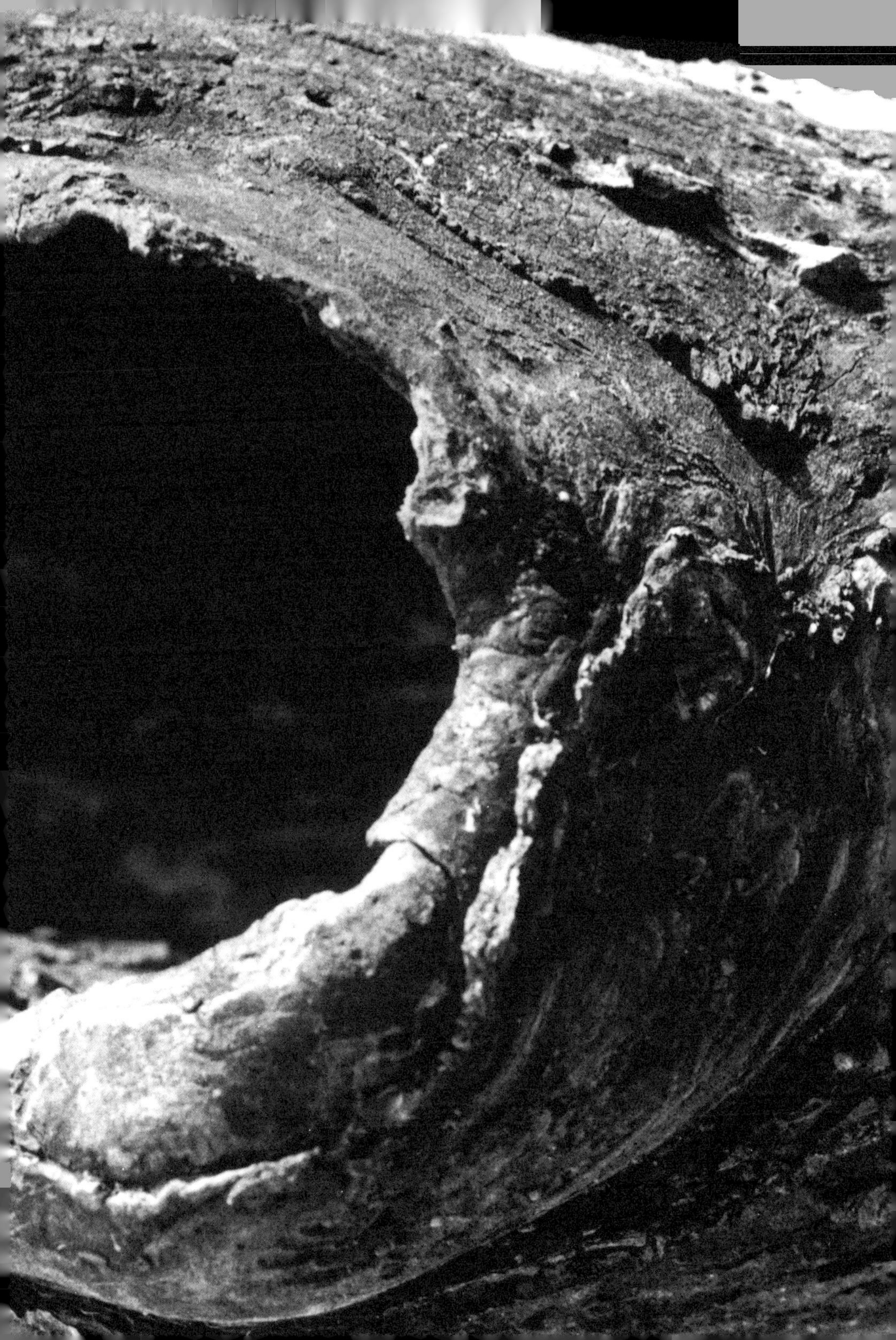

OLD TEACHER'S LAMENT

The children in the playground seem no older
than those who were in my classroom not
so long ago, no more than a decade or so.
In fact, isn't that one, the balding father
of a female child who already wears butt-floss
instead of a pair of shorts, isn't he a child
I had to throw out of class once or twice,
however long ago it was? That must be he,
now heavy and panting as he rings a horseshoe
or whatever it is and yells at his child to move.

I remember those years when I wondered
why I bothered to teach when, after a few years,
I wondered if I'd stand and throw up before
the day was over and the headmaster called
a meeting to insist we remember our responsibility
was for these kids, to get them into the world,
to form a world that just might work this time,
that just might hold back from tumbling
upon itself, leaving horseshoes to rust
between one yearly gathering and the next.

BLUES FOR A FRIEND

What is it you really want from me, my friend;
               what could you possibly want to know?
I wish I knew what it really is you want from me—
           what it is, my friend, you want to know.
              You may long ago have told me what it was,
              but it has disappeared and I am left in wonder.

And now I ask you again what it is you wanted to know—
               what you may, so long ago, have asked.
What is it you really would have liked to get from me;
               what it really is I should have got from you?
                I thought you said, in a hesitant voice, what it was,
              but it has long since disappeared from memory.

Dare I ask you once again what it is, from me,
               you might have wanted to know?
I'm not at all sure what it ever could have been
               I might have wanted then from you.
                And now there's much that I could learn from you,
              much that I have never known, and now would learn.

Would you at some point now know what it is
               you might have wanted to know?
Could you now know what the hell the question was
               I might back then have wanted to ask?
                Can you let me know what I should have said
              or what, in a song like this, I might still try to say?

Ah, my friend, time has slipped away and there
               is still too much I do not know.
Time has slipped away and I still wonder, my friend,
             what you may know that I will never know.
                Perhaps it's too late now and I shall never know
              whatever it is that we could never share.

BLUE ROCKER

I slipped in silence and only a little hesitancy
        back into my chair and groaned;
oh dear, I groaned, and slipped in uncomfortable silence
        to the very back of my chair.
    Then suddenly I heard your whispering voice and woke,
    wondering if that was really you whispering in the room.

But it didn't take long to slip back into the silence of the room
        and my comfortable old chair;
I slipped quickly to deep sleep in the back
        of my comfortable old rocker of a chair.
    Then, suddenly, I sat up to sounds you make,
    to a whisper somewhere in a corner of the room.

Now I was restless and couldn't fall asleep in the room,
        much less in my chair;
there was no way that I could fall asleep or even
        be able to read a book in my rocking chair.
    There was not a sound anywhere to be made,
    not by you or by anyone else in that deserted room.

And now I knew that I wouldn't fall asleep, not now,
        not in that old rocking chair;
not now, in a room full of silence when there was no sleep,
        no sleep at all in that old rocker of a chair.
    So I rose and searched for you through silence;
    searching, I wandered through the empty rooms.

So, without sleeping, I wandered through the day, until
        the last lingering of light;
and even as the room got dark again I wandered through
        the night, unable to sit in that old rocker.
    Through a long night full of silence, I waited
    to hear your sounds, apparently gone from the room.

BLUE SEARCH FOR THE TRUTH

It may be true, she said, but there's no way to prove it—
        even if it might be so;
no, no, there's no way you can prove it, even if there is
        a way to show it might be so.
    And now we need to pause and see just where we are;
    even if we find ourselves cursing at the truth.

And could it really be so, you said, as I tried to turn away—
        could she have been right?
No, no, if you or she were right, could you prove it?
        Could there really be a way to show it's so?
    We argued this what seems like decades ago,
    and chased the truth around a volume of possibilities.

Perhaps she's right, you said. Do you remember that?
        It's certainly a probability, you said.
Perhaps you are right, she said when I asked if she remembered;
        and all that you could say, was a quiet 'maybe.'
    By that time it was not even an argument, just something
    that you and she said when there was nothing else to say.

Why is it that, as age pulls out the plug and leaves us
        wondering just what we might have meant,
we feel a sudden remembrance and wonder just what
        we might have been getting at.
    By this time I can't remember what it was you said
    when I told you the sad things that she had said.

Perhaps I should have listened to what you said,
        so long ago that I can't remember what it was;
but I did listen, way back then, to what she said,
        and asked you what it was all about.
    But why, now, does the question rise again;
    and why, now, do we even care which of us said what?

BLUE REGRETS

I wanted to tell you what I heard as the sun came up,
            and I knew I had something to say;
Yes, just as the sun came up, I woke to tell you
            what I knew I had to say as darkness disappeared.
      But it was too late, for you were gone; the sun
      no sooner threw its light than you were gone.

I wanted to tell you how sorry I was for what I'd said
            the night before as darkness filled the room;
I had wanted, the night before, to tell you how very sorry
            I was. Or was it after the dark was fully here?
      But I couldn't remember just what it was I'd said,
      though it was something I wish I had not said.

Maybe it was when we woke about halfway
            through the night, in the dark;
maybe it was then, when we woke, that I said something
            I never should have said.
      I vaguely remember, you reached and touched my back,
      and we were awake again until I said something rude.

Was it really so rude? Was what I said something
            I never should have said?
Was it really so crude? Did I do something
            I never should have done?
      Was it something I did in the middle of the night,
      something I never should have said or done in the dark?

But when the sun came up, you were gone, without a note,
            with nothing to say about why you were gone.
You were gone by the time the sun came up, by the time
            the light had crossed the room.
      I looked around and found that you were gone,
      even as the sky turned blue with the sun and regrets.

WHERE MUSIC BEGINS

Professor Barnum gave me a chord
and told me to let it whisper with intensity
between five notes that Mozart
had chosen to take for an early start
to expectedly rough ends of exploration.

While Sidney Bechet on a tour through town
gave me one note and told me to see
how many ways I could play that note—
"growl it, smear it, flat it, sharp it, do anything
you want to it," he said. Just one note.

But where do I stop, I ask myself?
Just the other night, working
on a little Bach, I was aware
that it began with a single note and stopped
with a set of three, and faded away.

It's like the song I often hear
somewhere inside of me,
often just there; and I reach for it,
try to fill the room with a voice off balance,
even when I know where it should start and end.

Maybe that's what life is all about,
trying to find just where the balance is
for a sonata or wild jazz that growls,
trying to fill lingering emptiness
between where music begins and where it ends.

NOT SURE

I'm not at all sure what life is all about,
even if from time to time I think I am,
am arrogantly sure; but not for long,
for I wake and wander through another book
and catch my breath because it doesn't say
just what I thought for sure it was bound to say.
Or I revisit another town and see
a small collection I once had thought special,
unusual for a random town in the south;
but this trip left me wondering if what I saw
could possibly be what once had turned me on,
if those large nudes had always been so pink
and awkward; and now I am arrogantly sure
that two of the impressions are certainly fakes.

And now I need to reassure myself
that of course I can be sure, that all it takes
is a laugh that puts me back at ease, a laugh
at the awkward incarcerations of old age.
But would that be enough to make me sure
of just what life is really all about?
When I was 10, I simply went to work
and did whatever it was I was told to do,
and wondered why I had to scrub floors
and carry groceries to an old lady's car.
And then I tried to teach and found it okay
up to a point, but wondered what it's about;
and, yes, I write these poems, and always grin
and wonder if finally I've seen the point.

FRAGILE FRIENDSHIP

I tried to tell him what it was all about,
but he didn't want to hear, not then; and so
we went in different directions and lost touch—
until she left for someone else,
a rather awful guy; and he and I met again
on the street, on a bench outside the bookshop
where we sat and let our usual heavy breath
slow and soften in the spring afternoon.

"How long has it been?" I said, and he laughed
and I was afraid that, just for a moment,
I'd let an edge drop through the question;
but he laughed and pushed his cane aside
and reached to take my hand in his—
"It's been too long," I said; "I know," he said;
"but she was pushing me pretty hard and said
she should have run away with you."

I knew what she had said when her son was born
and he and I buried the placenta in the corn patch
and then drank too much of his home-made brew
and left the cleaning up to the local girl
whom I was living with, at least for awhile
in a shack—but that was 40 years before;
and, yes, we'd spent decades in arguments
back and forth in Vermont or Philadelphia.

And then he found another wife or two
and found a place for a few poems of mine
and came down when I was single to see
a show at our museum, or hear if my piano
was good enough for his new girl who played
at private clubs or elegant apartments
on the East Side where I was invited to read
a poem or two between her fugues.

JUST FRIENDS

"No. No," she said, staring straight beyond him;
"we're just old friends," and tried to smile at me,
but left a flush across the slope of her face and in her eye.
"It's ok," she said; "there's nothing else—we're friends."
And that's all, I thought, just friends? "I've been there,"
I said, wondering just what might be meant by the phrase
"just friends," which, actually, I've never used.
What could it have been, if she or he were just a friend?
What would be the other side of that? What's *just*
if one is judging rigorously what a friend might be?

I've had many friends who were not lovers, with whom
I never found myself in bed; but they were not *just* friends.
There was much more than that as we sat on the edge
and waited for the tide to rise or sat at the back
of the stage and wondered if the guest conductor
could hold it all together, if the young violinists
would remember that they were more than just friends,
that the very existence of their Bach depended on
the loving support that depended upon so much more
than a casual or passionate hour in bed.

WHAT MIGHT HAVE BEEN

How can I know what world might have been
if he and I had spent more time together,
back then, way back before I found a path
that finally became the path that I would take,
wandering among distant islands in search
of another stranger with whom I might explore
the hinges of life I never understood.

He's still there, somewhere out there where I
suspect he has opened gates I never found
with a key that only works on iron now rusted
by rising floods and a squeezing out of time;
and I am here, quietly here where flowers
hang through the afternoon with desperation
and memories of a rich passage from spring.

I cannot imagine what path he ended on,
not now, not after I have drawn his image
and left it lingering in these piles of words
that crowd dark shelves and line a path
on which he's never stumbled, though they fall
and splash in the quiet cove where his gray ghost
always seems to whisper fun reminders.

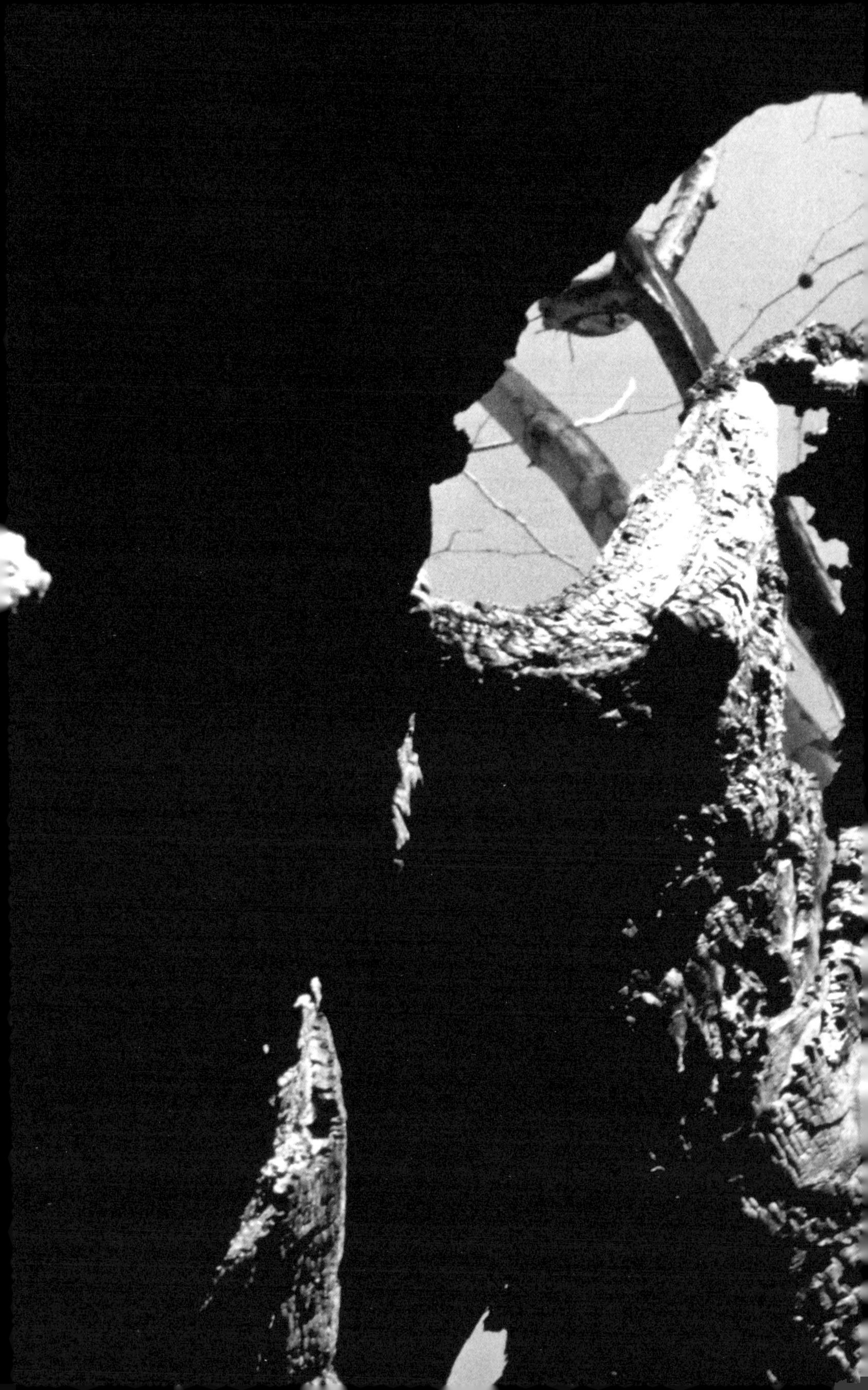

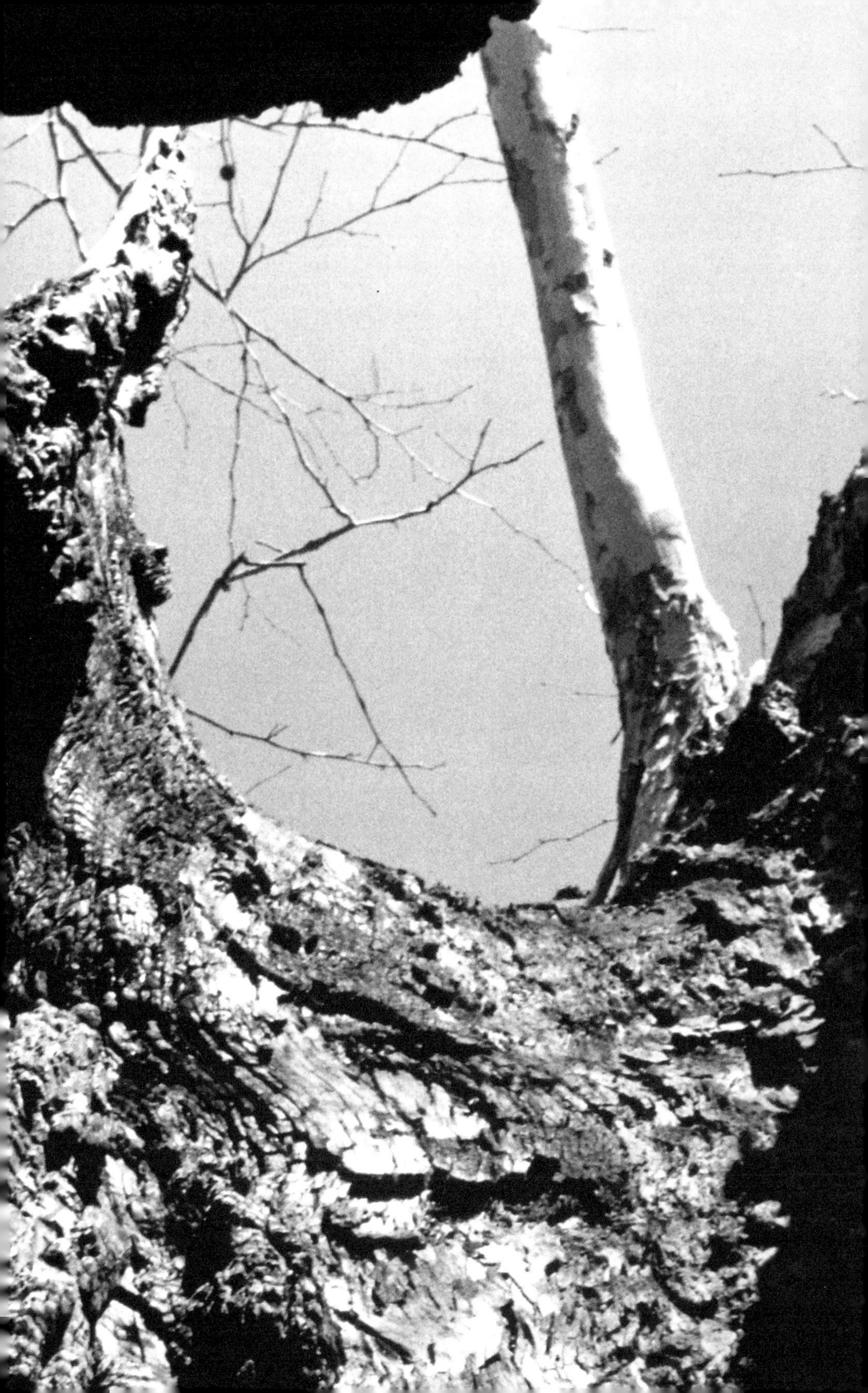

SHARING WITH A FRIEND

If we need anything…, you say. Well, come, my dear:
we always need something. Don't you? What is wonderful
is to feel there is someone who just might have something
we'll need at some time. After all, there are times
when I need to hear someone sing or play the piano —
and to smile while doing so, which is, after all, your gift:
to smile while being utilized, especially for music.

What's the weather…, you ask. Well, there was an inch
of snow when we woke, but it melted with a shy sun;
and now, as sun should set if it were anywhere about,
the snow is blowing increasingly large flakes; and by
the time I send this poem with hugs and many *miss-yous,*
the last light will fade and we'll not know
until morning what the weather has really been about.

All the paint…, you say. Well, I used to paint wall and trim:
and it was hard even when I was in my 40s; it hurt
in my 50s; and became impossible in my 60s. So I will not
offer to come running to help out, though I will send
lots of good wishes for survival. Will Brian help
with a fluid brush? You know, he's the second finest person
we've met down there. Gee, I wonder who's the finest!

GATOR THREATS

I

I remember a gator that slapped his heavy tail
in mud at the edge of the lake where my mother
had forbidden me to wander all by myself
and I did anyway and fell in fright from my bike
and had to hide that memory in the dark attic
where each year I stuffed away another sigh,
a little more removed from my genetic pile.

And now, at 80, I dig into that trunk
of rotting memories and wonder where
I might have ended up if I had not been
so secretive about the gator threats of the world
in the push I continue to make around a lake,
looking for a place where I can be myself
and risk the slap of a tail that's still so attractive.

II

I've had at times a number of friends who knew
what gators at the edge of the lake were about;
in fact they came at times so close to the edge
they disappeared, and I've not heard from them
in 50 years or more, though sometimes at night
I'll hear their favorite curse, sharp as the threat
that I was warned about and never believed.

And I will wake and wander around the house,
often ending in the attic where the boxes,
heavy and even stinky, wait for someone
to come and say, yes, that's what we want,
just that, to complete the arguments we thought
we had about the seriousness of the world,
the challenges we grab from gator threats.

DISMISSAL OF AN ATHEIST

His book sounds and feels like a book by those
devout Christian ministers and enthusiastic rabbis
I've had pushed on me for most of my life;
I've even read books by devout atheists,
out to convert us, that were just as uncomfortable.
The Christians claimed that the damned Jews
and unbelievers (atheists) were to blame
for all our ills and should be destroyed; yes,
that's what they were saying where I grew up;
and there were rabbis who wrote and preached
that not until Muslims were totally defeated
would peace be possible in their world;
and atheists said what Richard Dawkins says,
preaching as if atheism too were a religion.

With knowledge of these wars and others,
of the good and the horror done by Christians,
Muslims, Jews, and Unbelievers (and let's not forget
the horrors done by Buddhists and Taoists
and Nazis…)—after reading the works written
by all of these, and more, after training
in how to think and how to interrelate ideas,
I and most of the people I've known
(unfortunately not those in power) realize that,
yes, we may have to live an atheistic life,
but that atheists like Richard Dawkins are as intent
on destroying others as any Jew or Muslim
or Christian or *anti-others* we've ever known
or read about in the long or short lives we've had.

Some people need Judaism or Christianity
or Atheism because they have to be part of a group;
some have to say all representative sculptors are bad,
retrograde, a hindrance for the progress of art;
they say that unless we break down the tonality
of music we'll have nothing new. Many human beings
have long used selfish power to hold their own

and put down others, just as do many animals
that live in groups. For food, for gold, for oil,
for prestige (they think), for sex, they cut throats
of others, sometimes of others in their own tribes.
What we need are not destructive efforts
by such as Richard Dawkins; what we need are not
destruction of Muslims, Jews, Christians or their gods.

Many of us may or may not believe in these gods;
many of us out here only believe in the potential
of human kindness or the potential of human creativity
as apposed to human hate and destruction.
What we need are those moments when we reach
to touch each other with comfort and gentleness.
After all, Russians were as destructive when they
held atheistic belief in power as they were
when they were a Christian force or, and earlier,
a pantheistic force, as indeed were the Romans,
who brought the West together as Christians
and led us out to destroy the rest of the world.
My best friend was a black Baptist who was hung
in a pine tree by a white Methodist sheriff.

We've said it before: it's the damned human beings,
some of them, not all of them…. It's just too bad
that, for those who need it, there can't be
a peaceful god or energy or idea. It's too bad
that, even if we dislike certain kinds of art
or art forms, we can't just turn away and believe
and create what we wish. It's too bad we can't have
a little more love in the world (by whatever name
it's called) and a lot less hate and destruction;
but with more people like Richard Dawkins,
it will soon be too late and there will only be
more destructiveness. This is indeed
"the foul rag and bone shop of the heart"
about which a great modern poet warned us.

A BIRTHDAY

In disapproval, I have little tolerance for weddings
or birthdays or funerals; and both of my weddings
were full of avoidances, one marked, on a far island,
by a gay hunk playing Buxtehude on a small pump organ
where half the keys would make no connective sound
and the other with a Salvation Army captain, long pregnant
and in process of becoming Jewish, playing on her guitar
and singing loudly, "I Wish I Were Single Again."

Nor can I remember when either of my daughters
has a birthday or some special disaster to commemorate.
I mean I mess their names with others or even my own:
What's he called who's writing this poem to whom?
But by writing myself notes and marking a band-aid
with the date, I remembered yesterday was Andrea's,
which she is as forgetful of as I, and we ended
having the loveliest day either of us could remember.

We wake at some unidentified time as a new sun
glitters on Assateague Bay at the back of our property
and spreads out across Chincoteague Bay beyond windows
out front where we stir awake in awe of light. Yes, we say,
we'll go and drive south with camera and car-music,
pen and pad, after first stopping at skinny Rita's for eggs
and bacon and a laugh with hugs—always the best way
to begin a day, especially a day with no predetermined map.

And then, we go down a back road and pass through
an almost deserted NASA base and through vast fields
of dying corn or still-green tomatoes by decayed houses
where Andrea pauses to expose film for a future book;
until after a while we decide to swing into a small
18th-century village where resurrection has been tried
without success—which is just as well since it gives subject
to a camera looking for passage of a world that was.

For a late lunch we go into the only café in the village,
Club Car, where decor, waitresses, and food date
from decades earlier—wonderful and barely edible.
Even heavy guys in mismatched booths are from then,
even if unborn then; it is a Woolworth I ate in as a kid;
though now there is a john in a storage room corner
where there is also a door into an almost hidden bar,
pool room, gambling room, without a person to be seen.

Then we wander on through ruins of motels to a village
full of faded mansions, a good health food and wine store
where we buy stacks of stuff for our new kitchen;
and the very nice clerk says she is going to return north
to get a job with regular pay; and, again, Andrea wanders
stranded streets to take photographs of 5 or 6 blocks
where no one moves, where no window reflects life—
all gone, leaving small freighters and boxcars rotting.

Two restaurants, once good, have closed; a movie house
sits vacant but with a fading notice of something coming up;
and two out of every three stores is closed, junk piled high
in dusty windows; though a beat-up hardware store
has an aging, well-spoke lady who shells butter beans
every night and all morning and sells them at a few bucks
for a couple of pounds and probably makes a better profit
than on shovels hidden in dark corners of the dark back.

With a car full of peaches and beans and whisks, we head
back though deserted shore roads to our bayside escape,
but not without stopping in our own village to get a serving
of the darkest, richest 'marsh mud' chocolate ice cream,
stuffed in a home-made cone that you have to imagine.
"After all," we tell ourselves, we who never celebrate such days,
"it is Andrea's birthday;" and, as a matter of fact, we tell
each other, it's the best birthday we've ever celebrated.

MEMORIES IN AN OLD ROCKER

No, not that, I'm too old for that;
of course there was a time…, oh yes;
but those times are gone and I sit
in a window at the top of the house
and watch time fly. Time fly?
I see yellow and gray autumn leaves
slip across the garden clusters;
but that's not what I mean, not at all.

No, even if it sounds like it,
this is not what I mean when I say
those times are gone, finally,
even when I remember the fun we had
that's also gone, even as the leaves
dry and crush in piles that need
to be left to rot and become
the best of rich compost for roses.

No, whatever it is you may think,
you've slipped away from what truth
might be for why I sit quietly
here in an old rocking chair
and sigh at the lost passageway
that could have gone out there
beyond that pile of leaves
or up there from where they fell.

No, that's not really what I mean,
not at all; I am still thinking of those
who died or drifted away like leaves,
who rotted and left memories
like rose hips on the edge of time.
No, while I can, I shall remember;
I shall sit here between two windows
and watch daylight darken and fall.

NOTES FROM BACH

For too long now I sit and wait
and wonder who will ring the bell
that says to come on down, it's time;
and it is. For months, I've sat up here
and tried to read one book or another
and wondered which would give me comfort
of one kind or another, just here
where I sit and listen for falling notes
to which I've listened, in one form or another,
for almost 80 years—though now
it isn't I who digs for them
from the black piano in the music room.
No, now I put on a disc and listen
and sigh that these are not the notes
I shared with old ladies at their clubs
or lovely blondes at school assemblies.
But they're still from Bach, rising and falling,
reaching into a world that made
the hairs on the back of my neck tremble
as if it were part of a gesture of sex
in a world I knew so little about;
but now I wait to know if the notes
will pull up in sudden confrontation
with a world that seems to frame my heart
in a crumbled frame that leaves me stumbling
as if this is it, if this quiet afternoon
is all these notes have left to offer.

NOT TIME

It's not time yet; it can't be—not yet;
we've just got the seeds ready.
Nothing is up, except the memory
I have of what we called *a hard on*.
You remember, at least I hope you do,
when seeds sprouted and we were 12,
or I was; and older friends
were dying in fields of North Africa,
and I was in camp in North Carolina
where a slightly older guy taught riding
and would die as cavalry headed for Berlin;
but now he patted himself on the crotch
and said "Play a little with it,
just there, when you get back to the tent.
It's fun; and good for you." And it was,
fun, that is, though he couldn't have enjoyed
it too often, since it was soon time
for him to go—and he did, while I drag on
for another 70 years, watching seeds
sprout with fresh lettuce, even as I
remember my uncle's drunken tales
of armies blasting through muddy fields,
pushing aside whatever time
there might have been for something fun
in a tent where seeds spin and don't sprout.

TALES FOR ME

Though much from the past appears in the dark of night,
        I still can't find the image of a birth—
it's simply gone and has been gone for decades,
        except I do remember words to describe
what is said to have happened when a surgeon thrust
        his forceps into my mother's womb and grabbed
my head and twisted it and left an eye
        scarred, distressed and lingering without function.

It was just bad eyesight, nothing I thought about
        even as I learned to read *Robinson Crusoe*
with the help of grandfather, teaching me to read,
        preparing me to leave as he left,
Crusoe and he, around the globe, restless
        on a wooden boat finally left rotting until
it sank at a dock where fishermen remembered me,
        a small boy he carried in his arms until the end.

That was his end, not mine; mine still lingers,
        decades later, in spite of the times I was told
that I would never make it, that by the end
        of a year or 10 I would be dead, washed up
on one of the islands my grandfather wandered around,
        leaving the family to slip away as my father did,
not in pain, for I never remember if there was pain;

In and out of bed, in and out of a closed room
        where piles of books lingered on the edge of a bed
as if they were the island house where grandfather
        lived while waiting to die; year after year
I read whatever books I could find and remember
        in the privacy of my own memory his tales
that no one else would ever tell; they were
        for me, he said, for no one else—for me.

ARGUMENTS

1

"*Yes*," I shout, and shout again with a *Yes*;
while "*No*," he whispers, "*No*, it can't be so."
"Why not?" I say and try to lower my voice;
"There's no other way it could be except that."
"Exactly," he says, turning to see if I
am ready to listen to what he'd like to say;
or if he should let it drop until later,
until we are ready to balance the *Yes* with a *No*
that might bring back a sudden grin or smile,
a smile we often share when *No* is not
at war with an angry *Yes* that flops around
and tries to anchor itself to a calmer moment.
Or is it he who calls with a vociferous *Yes*
while I'm the one who whispers a half-blind *No*?

2

The arguments that old friends have as they age
and wonder just where it all will end, as it will,
and wonder why the sound the other makes
so drenches the dry dependencies of hope,
are riches that linger on the edge of a cliff.
It's not the polished surface of the cliff
that pulls me out across a morning's hope;
it's clatter of treasure settling in the sun,
memory and hope that only a friend can bring—
a *Yes* that's polished like a silver spoon,
a *No* that fades like a golden toe of Buddha
that we might have known when we were young
and didn't know what arguments become
when they drift around in monosyllabic tones.

3

A *Yes* can show approval of the dark
that might have left our generation to fall
into the splendors of a dream; while *No*,
even in a whisper, can pull us down
into the world we never thought we'd miss,
that scared us shitless when we were kids.
You remember, you saw it from a mountain top,
while I was chased around the lake
where gators waited with their own harsh sound.
We got through that, you and I, and now,
in words we still will push across the day,
with passion or with fear, we laugh and wonder
if we will ever really know just which
are words that might bring us into the light.

4

You're the *Yes* man, my friend, and carry a laugh
beyond the one I lost in trying to find
a reason for the *No* that's kept me going,
that's left me hanging on the edge with a word
that leaps across the mud where gators cough.
Now you are there, wherever that may be,
and I am here trying to figure out
just what the word should be when we decide
we really have the *Yes* that hugs a *No*
that one of us prefers or thinks we do,
listening in the wind that blows all day
and calls us to the edge of what we are,
a couple of old guys who love to argue
about which word will keep us going strong.

WORD FOR ANOTHER POEM

I know for you *word* is something else,
not just a part of syntax giving us
another phrase that might help a poem
sing itself through a hunk of time.

I stumble when I think of that word
that gets another book started once again;
damn, I think, there are 87 words
in his first paragraph that only add to one.

That's what I've heard you say: it all drops
to one, you say, ending with "in the beginning;"
I read these words and play with them
at night, and have no trouble taking them away.

I take them to the edge of another blank sheet,
as a poem that wants to dump the preacher
who never wanted to hear what a child might say
who had just learned that words can lead.

Across the restless night they led and satisfied,
being alive beside the pillow in the morning
with other words that pull another word
and probably come a little closer to you.

But you had not been born, not yet,
not for a long while yet until we come close
and share just what another word may mean
when another poem echoes on the page.
no, not pain, just the blur of what might come.

AFTER 80 YEARS

Can I, after 80 years, look out at distant hills
and see, beyond the worlds I thought I knew
and know, with great reluctance, that what
I thought was a world of exploration and love
was really the explosive devices left by wars
to wash up and undermine the world we thought
we'd left for generations of our children?

How can I watch the dark clouds of storms
repel the light I sought to hold within my sight,
just there, see, between me and where the dark
might have fallen at any moment, leaving me
to wonder how I held onto expectations I've held
for all these decades I have actually enjoyed,
in spite of what I always feared would be?

And even when the sky is blue can we expect
to see the sun fall with brilliance in the west,
can we ignore the storm clouds in the east,
explosions we hear in broadcasts of angry days;
can we try, at least for an afternoon,
to escape and let fall the pained consciousness
as we lift a glass of wine to a quiet fall of the day?

For decades I have tried to rise and fall and see
what there might be beyond the windows
I've waited in, beyond the windows that open
to the clarity of an afternoon, the stormy
falling of light that I depended upon, the hope
I tried to share with friends I held to during
this passage of time I've found my way through.

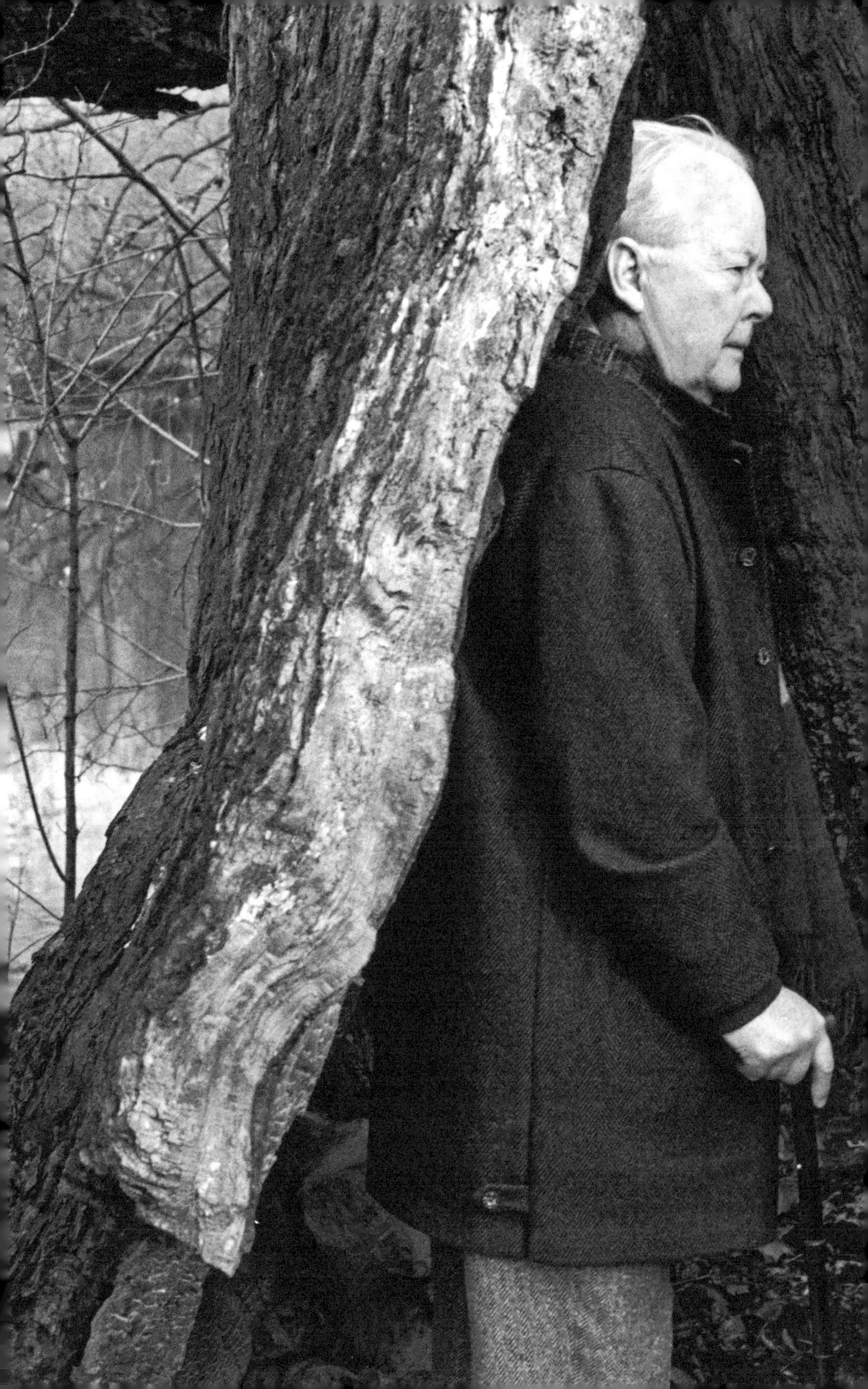

A Brief Biography

Just before I began this volume, after almost 75 years of writing poetry, I was wondering if those writing days weren't over; but then Andrea and I started to spend more time in a pine forest down on Chincoteague Island and to watch the sun sink into the bay and to eat fresh fish every day of the week. That, plus listening to retired whores at the local tavern, pushed me back into the inner world of rhythmic words and lines that could be piled together like small sculptures or brief bagatelles.

So, after a year, here is another volume; and it isn't the only one finished, started or rewritten this year; but now, well into my 80th year, I have to wonder…: if I'm not around when you read one of the poems, enjoy it and remember me even if we never met.

BOOKS OF POEMS BY WILLIAM HOLLIS

Early Encounters

Midlife Encounters

Letters And Voices From The Steppes

Scenes From An Old Album

Sketches For A Mayan Odyssey

Sonata Sonnets

Las Espinas

13 x 13 x 13

Dark Encounter In Mid Air

Poem-Chanting Tower

Lilith & The Blues

Gathering Of Wanderers

With Others

With The Self

Venetian Passage

Poems From Letters

Heart of a Tree

At the Forge

BOOKS OF PHOTOGRAPHS BY ANDREA BALDECK

The Heart Of Haiti

Talismanic

Venice A Personal View

Touching The Mekong

Closely Observed

Presence Passing

Himalaya: Land Of The Snow Lion

*Design and production of this book were managed by
Veronica Miller & Associates, Haverford, Pennsylvania.
Production supervision was provided by Peter Philbin.
The book was printed by Brilliant Graphics, Exton, Pennsylvania
and was bound by The Riverside Group, Rochester, New York.*